HONEY

Edible

Series Editor: Andrew F. Smith

EDIBLE is a revolutionary series of books dedicated to food and drink that explores the rich history of cuisine. Each book reveals the global history and culture of one type of food or beverage.

Already published

Apple Erika Janik *Banana* Lorna Piatti-Farnell
Barbecue Jonathan Deutsch and Megan J. Elias
Beef Lorna Piatti-Farnell *Beer* Gavin D. Smith
Brandy Becky Sue Epstein *Bread* William Rubel
Cake Nicola Humble *Caviar* Nichola Fletcher
Champagne Becky Sue Epstein *Cheese* Andrew Dalby
Chillies Heather Arndt Anderson *Chocolate* Sarah Moss
and Alexander Badenoch *Cocktails* Joseph M. Carlin
Curry Colleen Taylor Sen *Dates* Nawal Nasrallah
Doughnut Heather Delancey Hunwick *Dumplings* Barbara Gallani
Edible Flowers Constance L. Kirker and Mary Newman
Eggs Diane Toops *Fats* Michelle Phillipov *Figs* David C. Sutton
Game Paula Young Lee *Gin* Lesley Jacobs Solmonson
Hamburger Andrew F. Smith *Herbs* Gary Allen *Honey* Lucy M. Long
Hot Dog Bruce Kraig *Ice Cream* Laura B. Weiss *Lamb* Brian Yarvin
Lemon Toby Sonneman *Lobster* Elisabeth Townsend
Melon Sylvia Lovegren *Milk* Hannah Velten *Moonshine* Kevin R. Kosar
Mushroom Cynthia D. Bertelsen *Nuts* Ken Albala *Offal* Nina Edwards
Olive Fabrizia Lanza *Onions and Garlic* Martha Jay
Oranges Clarissa Hyman *Pancake* Ken Albala
Pasta and Noodles Kantha Shelke *Pie* Janet Clarkson
Pineapple Kaori O' Connor *Pizza* Carol Helstosky
Pomegranate Damien Stone *Pork* Katharine M. Rogers
Potato Andrew F. Smith *Pudding* Jeri Quinzio *Rice* Renee Marton
Rum Richard Foss *Salad* Judith Weinraub *Salmon* Nicolaas Mink
Sandwich Bee Wilson *Sauces* Maryann Tebben *Sausage* Gary Allen
Seaweed Kaori O'Connor *Soup* Janet Clarkson
Spices Fred Czarra *Sugar* Andrew F. Smith *Tea* Helen Saberi
Tequila Ian Williams *Truffle* Zachary Nowak
Vodka Patricia Herlihy *Water* Ian Miller
Whiskey Kevin R. Kosar *Wine* Marc Millon

Honey

A Global History

Lucy M. Long

REAKTION BOOKS

Published by Reaktion Books Ltd
Unit 32, Waterside
44–48 Wharf Road
London N1 7UX, UK
www.reaktionbooks.co.uk

First published 2017

Printed and bound in China by 1010 Printing International Ltd

A catalogue record for this book is available from the British Library

ISBN 978 1 78023 733 6

Contents

Introduction

Stickiness, sweetness and bees. Those are the associations with honey that many of us have. My own memories of honey are tied to childhood visits to my father's family in the Appalachian mountains of western North Carolina. We always stopped at one of the many makeshift roadside stands to purchase jars of honey. Local and home processed, the raw honey in the jars usually contained pieces of floating honey-comb, which we treated like chewing gum. Sourwood and clover tended to be the most common flavours, but nectars from locust, linn and poplar trees and numerous wildflowers also flavoured the local honeys. Everyone seemed to keep bees; wooden hives were a frequent part of the landscape, and a jar of honey was on every kitchen table. The honey was dribbled over warm cornbread or biscuits fresh out of the oven. We would eat with our fingers, our hands dripping with melted butter and honey – sticky fingers were an expected result, along with a full and satisfied tummy.

As I grew older and was fortunate to travel the world, I found honey to be a constant – usually as a sweetener or a flavouring for pastries and other foods. It was also stirred into drinks, hot tea usually, and used to soothe sore throats. Honey's ubiquity, though, almost disguises its significance.

Sourwood honey from the mountains of western North Carolina.

It has played a major role in the nourishment and health of humankind from ancient civilizations up to the present, not only as a food, but as a medicine, topical ointment, preservative and an energizer; it has even been used as an embalming fluid and adhesive.

Historically, honey featured in mythology and religious rituals. Considered a food for the gods, it also played a role in some creation stories. Even today, honey features in language, the arts and popular culture. Its sweetness is associated with romance and affection, and the word 'honey' is often used as a term of endearment. It can also refer to truthful and honest speech, and when associated with food, health or cosmetic products, it tends to represent the best of the natural world.

What is honey, though? According to the Merriam-Webster Dictionary, it is 'a sweet viscid material elaborated out of the nectar of flowers in the honey sac of various bees'. It is not a very appetizing description, nor is the process of creating honey very appealing. Bees collect nectar from flowering plants, swallowing it through their straw-like probosces into a special sac, called a 'honey stomach', where an enzyme is added that causes inversion, transforming the complex sugars of the nectar into simpler ones. That mixture is then regurgitated to other bees in the hive, who also consume it and then regurgitate it again into honeycomb cells. The bees then rapidly flap their wings, fanning the honeycombs and causing the water in the nectar to evaporate and turning it into honey, which is stored to be used as food for the bees. Considering the size of honeybees, it comes as no surprise that a lone bee over its entire lifetime can make only one-twelfth of a teaspoon of honey. The honey that we consume represents the cooperative effort of hundreds, if not thousands, of bees.

The history of honey is intertwined with the history of bees – of mankind's beliefs about them, of attempts to find and gather honey from them, and the strategies utilized to contain and cultivate bees so as to control honey production and harvest it more easily. Bees themselves have been the subject of literature, art, music and other imaginative pursuits, as well as the focus of an occupation and hobby – one of the earliest cave paintings, dating from 8000 BC, shows bees surrounding human figures gathering honey, and some of the first printed works in the Western world were about beekeeping.

Honey is a complicated subject. Bees 'manufacture' other products along with honey, and these are frequently found literally mixed in with the honey or associated with it: 'bee pollen' (pellets of pollen formed by bees in the hive and used as a source of protein), propolis (a resinous substance collected by bees from trees and turned into 'glue' for their hives), royal jelly (a bee secretion used to feed the larvae and the queen bee) and wax from the honeycomb. These have had a variety of uses throughout history, including culinary ones.

Humans are not the only creatures to appreciate honey. Some of those that have a particular affinity for it are named accordingly – the honeyguide bird, honey badger – and others, such as bears, have reputations for being extremely fond of the substance. Honey is used in the naming of plants – for example, the honey locust tree and honeysuckle – and for some cultural ideas and traditions, including honey buckets used to collect 'night soil' and the term 'honeymoon'.

Perhaps one of the fascinations of honey is that it can be consumed both raw, straight from the bees producing it, and in culinary concoctions. As 'material considered appropriate for ingestion', food is a cultural construction (that is, the definition of what can and should be eaten develops within each culture and can change over time). As such, food is usually 'worked' in some way, to use the anthropologist Claude Lévi-Strauss' concept that cultures turn raw materials into something that fits the category of food. Honey, however, can be eaten straight from the hive, by hand, and even surrounded by bees. It is turned into food partly through the rituals surrounding it, the material artefacts containing it and its uses in the culinary arts, yet it retains a connection to its raw state, and is often best unchanged. In a way, honey offers a bridge between our civilized state and our 'natural' one. In the same way, it can move us from today's modern world with its industrialized food system to a more natural, organic way of life that connects us to experiences and wisdom from the past and from a diversity of cultures.

Putto eating honey, 1750, by Joseph Anton Feuchtmayer.

Today, there are concerns about the future of honey. Honeybees are in crisis in the u.s. and Europe, and there are doubts about their survival in many countries, such as Turkey. Not only does the loss of bee colonies make honey more expensive, but the role of bees as pollinators means that the sustainability of many agricultural crops crucial to our food supply is at stake. In addition, commercially produced honey is sometimes blended with other substances, and some forms of modern processing dilute its healthful properties, so that honey itself can no longer be turned to as a beneficial and healthy part of our diet. At the same time, beekeeping – and honey collecting – is a growing cottage industry and popular hobby. Tied to a number of social trends, beekeeping reflects a turn to self-sufficiency, the do-it-yourself movement and the revival of older lifestyles and skills, as well as a renewed respect for natural, seasonal foods and tastes. As a result, honey seems to be re-entering modern food cultures. The more we learn about this sweet substance, the more we can appreciate it – and treasure its worth, history and possible uses, as sticky as those may be.

I

Honey's Sweet History

Honey is a thick, sweet, syrupy substance made by bees from the nectar of flowers. It has a natural history tied to the bees that produce it and a cultural history linking humans to both the honey and the bees. Honey-producing bees were originally located in Central, South and Southeast Asia, Europe and northern Africa, as well as in Central America. Since honey is found naturally in the wild, does not spoil in its raw state and can be consumed with little to no processing, it was a staple of early cultures in those areas, not only as a food, but as medicine, tonic and preservative, and it was frequently associated with religious beliefs and ceremonial practices. As such, it has played a significant role in humanity's past, contributing to the survival of various groups and, in some cases, perhaps even changing the course of history. Although its function has shifted and it is now considered more of a supplemental sweetener, it is still important in the foodways of many cultures.

The hunting and 'domestication' of bees similarly has a long history. It was not only honey that was sought, but other bee products. Humans used the wax from the combs that bees built to store their larvae to make a variety of things, notably candles and seals. Propolis, a resinous substance collected by trees and turned into 'glue' for their hives, could be a medical sealant and salve for wounds and abscesses. ollen – the pellets formed by the hive worker bees from flower pollen brought back by foraging bees – is high in nutrients and protein and was used by humans as a dietary supplement. Royal jelly, similarly, is valued for its assumed high nutritional qualities; it is the substance secreted by bees that is fed to all larvae for several days, and then solely to the larvae designated to be the queen. Some cultures even eat the bee larvae.

The use of the bees themselves to pollinate desired crops has a long history. Some of the earliest records created by man – cave drawings, pottery, oral traditions and various writings – give accounts of people gathering honey and looking after the bees that produced it, suggesting the significance of the substance in the politics, economies, agriculture and religions of those cultures. The study of bees fascinated some of the

Working bees in a beehive.

earliest philosophers and artists and has today developed into the science of apiology.

The Natural History of Honey

Part of honey's history is the story of the creature that produces it: the honeybee. Honey is actually produced by several varieties of bees – totalling some 20,000 species – but only the honey made by the species *Apis mellifera* (also called the Western honeybee) is consumed by humans. The honeybee produces honey from nectar and pollen collected from flowering plants; the resulting watery substance is then dehydrated by the bees beating their wings over it. Bees also pollinate plants as they collect this nectar, so a historical aside to honey is the history of agriculture. Through pollination, honeybees made certain crops viable, and these were then cultivated in regions with strong honeybee populations. Today, the bees are 'managed' in order to support those crops, such as commercially grown almonds and blueberries in the u.s.

Bees themselves are thought to have originated in South or Southeast Asia around 40 million years ago and to have spread from there, although another authority dates their evolution from wasps to 125 million years ago.[1] Entomologists think that *Apis mellifera* is about 300,000 years old and developed in northern Africa. The bees then spread in the wild to surrounding areas, eventually evolving into nine species. The honeybee or *Apis* genus is then further divided according to nesting behaviour. Each species thrives in different environments, from deserts to tropical rainforests to cold tundra. The dwarf-sized *Apis florea* and *Apis andreniformis*, which continue to exist today, include several subgenera. The species each make their nests out of a single comb of honey. The species

Apis dorsata, or giant honeybee (within the subgenus *Megapis*), is native to South and Southeast Asia. Notorious for their aggressiveness and deadly stings, they build their nests high up in trees or on cliffs. A member of this particular giant species, the Himalayan honeybee (*Apis dorsata laboriosa*) – the largest of all honeybees – builds huge open nests. The other five species of honeybee build their nests in cavities (in trees, rock cliffs or hives); these are *Apis cerana*, *Apis koschevnikovi*, *Apis nuluensis*, *Apis nigrocincta* and *Apis mellifera*. The last is the honeybee that is most commonly known, and further divides into three primary subspecies: African, Eastern European and Western European. The Western European honeybee, the 'agricultural darling', has been the most domesticated by humans and has been central to pollinating modern crops as well as producing honey and wax.[2]

An infamous type of bee, the Africanized honeybee, is not a natural species, but is essentially an escaped science experiment that had been developed in Brazil. Known as 'killer bees', they are a hybrid of the European and African species, bred to be resilient to a tropical climate but still capable of producing honey, which native species are unable to do in viably large quantities. These adapted bees are larger and more aggressive than the honeybee and have been known to kill animals and humans. Although some fear their possible spread northwards and have called for their eradication, Brazilian beekeepers have learned to both protect themselves and work with the bees.

Humans learned to manage honeybees as early as 4,000 to 5,000 years ago, and took hives with them as they travelled. In this way, different species were introduced to new regions. The Western honeybee was particularly favoured in Europe. At the end of the fifteenth century, Spanish explorers were surprised to find indigenous people in Central

America keeping bees and harvesting honey, although the native bee seems to have been a much smaller variety. Honeybees were also taken by early settlers to North America in 1622. Although the first few colonies of bees died, they eventually became established, with some bees escaping and spreading to the Great Plains. They were taken west across the Rocky Mountains, first by Mormon settlers to Utah in the 1840s, then introduced into California during the 1850s by ship voyages around South America.[3] Similarly, European honeybees were brought to Australia in the 1820s by European settlers who wanted to ensure they had a supply of honey in their new home. The bees thrived there, with many colonies going 'feral' and establishing themselves in the wild. Today, honeybees and honey collecting occur throughout the world as both a home hobby and an industry. Commercial production of honey is a significant contributor to the economies of a number of nations as well as to numerous small-scale producers. The top honey-producing countries in 2005 varied according to different measures and were spread across the globe, but usually included China, Turkey, Ukraine, the USA, the Russian Federation, Argentina, Mexico, India, Iran and New Zealand.

The Cultural History of Honey

Although the exact nature of honeybees' relationship to honey was not understood until the seventeenth century, humans have been making use of it for thousands of years. Cave paintings from the eastern coast of Spain dating to 8,000 years ago show figures collecting honey from a cliff, and archaeological evidence suggests that honey was known in Europe as far back as 10,000 years ago. Honey vessels found

Man of Bicorp, Paleolithic rock painting of honey-gathering from a wild nest on a cliff. Gatherers used a rope ladder and basket, as is still done today in some cultures. Found in Cuevas de la Araña, Spain. The painting is estimated to be 8,000 years old.

in Georgia in Eastern Europe are 5,000 years old, mentions of honey have been discovered in cuneiform writings from Sumeria and Babylonia from as early as 2100 BC, and references to the substance are recorded in ancient Indian and Egyptian texts.[4] There is also evidence of honey being used by the early Chinese, Indians and Mayans as well as in areas of Africa. Honey's history as a part of human culinary culture is ancient and rich.

Origin Myths

For centuries, humans did not know how honey actually came into being. Colourful myths developed around it, and it was thought to be a divine substance, or a gift from the gods. It is no wonder, then, that it often carried symbolic meaning and was used in religious rituals, frequently as an offering to the gods. Some of these associations have continued into the present, with honey featuring in a number of religious holiday and ceremonial foods. Also, until the seventeenth century, bees were thought to be sexless, and to somehow self-create (autogenesis), which led to the bee's many diverse symbolic associations, such as representing the power of the gods, fertility, chastity, orderliness and obedience.

Ancient Egyptians believed that honey came from the gods, particularly their primary god, Ra (also spelled 'Re'),

Egyptian hieroglyph of a bee, used as a symbol of royalty and of Egypt, from a tomb for King Intef in Luxor, c. 2100 BCE.

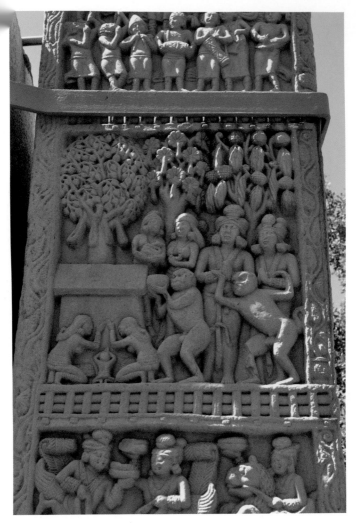

Stone relief in Sanchi Town, northeast India, 1st century BCE, referencing the legend of the monkey offering honey to Buddha when he was meditating in the forest.

and was collected by bees, which were then deemed to sacred manifestations of the gods and used as a symbol power. Translations of writings found on the Salt Papyru show how honey was considered to have a divine origin, and was an appropriate gift for the gods:

> The god Re wept and his tears fell to the ground and were turned into bees. The bees began to build and were active on all flowers of every kind belonging to the vegetable kingdom. Thus wax came into being and thus was created honey.[5]

Honey was used for embalming the dead, and it was placed in tombs for the deceased to enjoy in their afterlife. Royalty, who were believed to be the incarnations of gods on earth, were anointed with honey, and a hieroglyph of a bee represented the king of lower Egypt.

Ancient Semitic cultures believed honey to be a gift of the earth mother Astarte, the goddess of fertility, maternity and love (and, surprisingly, war). Early civilizations understood that honey represented fertility, of both the land and the people: 'As the land flows with milk and honey, so life-giving fluids flow from the genitals of men and women.'[6] It was often used to represent the Promised Land.

Honey was similarly associated with the gods in ancient India. In the 1,028 sacred hymns of the Vedic scriptures dating from 1500 BC, many frequently mention honey (*madhu* in Sanskrit) and claim that it came from the clouds. They use the name 'Madhava' (meaning 'honey-born ones') for the gods Vishnu, Krishna and Inra, and call honey the food of the gods. Honey was presented as a source of life and protection, and was therefore given as a gift to newborn males. 'I give thee this honey food so that the gods may protect thee, and

ou mayst live a hundred autumns in this world.'[7] Bees
[f]ermore were seen as liaisons between gods and men, and
[hon]ey was often used in offerings to the gods. This has car-
[ri]ed over into Buddhism as well as other cultures influenced
[b]y Indian culture and Hinduism. In Thailand, for example,
honey is ritually offered in acknowledgement of the honeycomb that a monkey gave to the Buddha when he needed
strength while seeking enlightenment.[8]

Similar legends abounded in ancient Greece, where
honey (*melis*) was again thought to come from the clouds.
It was considered a food of the gods, endowing them with

Wall painting at a monastery in Laos showing the legend of a monkey
offering honey to Buddha, photographed in 2006.

Greek vase showing men stung by bees.

immortality, and apparently consumed as nectar, mead or in ambrosia (ἀ-βροτός) – the prefix ἀ- means 'not', while βροτός (*brotos*) translates as 'mortals' (in other words, 'not for mortals'). It was given by the gods to humans when Dionysus, the son of Zeus and Semele, directed bees to fill a hollow tree in a forest with honey after a night of partying with the satyrs. Bees also came from the gods, specifically Zeus, who turned a beautiful girl named Melissa (whose name comes from the Greek word for honey, *meli*) into a bee. She then fed him milk and honey. Bees were called 'Melissae' and were 'caretakers, confidantes, and co-conspirators of the gods'. They could lead pilgrims to the Oracle at Delphi.[9] Homer, in the *Iliad* and

A 4,000-year-old kernos of the early Cycladic III period, from Melos in Greece, thought to be an offerings cup for honey and oats.

the *Odyssey*, probably written sometime around the eighth century BC, refers to both bees and honey as divine.

Even those Greeks who tried to be more scientific by observing the bees at work did not realize that bees made honey. The philosopher Aristotle (384–322 BC) experimented with beekeeping and included his observations in his *Historia animalium* (History of Animals) and *De generatione animalium* (Generation of Animals). He insisted, though, that 'the honey is what falls from the air, especially at the risings of the stars, and when the rainbow descends . . . it fetches in what falls from the air.'[10]

The Roman poet Virgil (70–19 BC) claimed that honey was 'heaven-borne, the gift of air'. (Like others, he also thought that bees did not produce offspring, but harvested their babies from flowers or sprang from the carcasses of lions and bulls.) Pliny the Elder, in his first-century AD *Natural History*, wrote about honey: 'whether this is the perspiration of the sky or a sort of saliva of the stars or the moisture of the air purging itself . . . it brings with it the great pleasure of its heavenly nature.'[11] The Romans offered honey to Proserpina, the goddess of spring and queen of the underworld, as it was intended to appease her and to encourage her to appear on earth as a harbinger of spring, rather than as volcanic lava.

Islamic texts also employed divine imagery, describing paradise as having rivers of wine, milk and honey. In contrast, though, the Qu'ran states that Allah told bees to make honey for humans, giving them a natural medicine: 'There comes from within [the bee] a beverage of many colors, in which there is healing for men.'[12]

Whatever beliefs were held about the origin of honey, it was significant enough for humankind to make records of it. One of the oldest-known cave paintings – from the Cuevas de la Araña (Spider Caves) in Valencia, Spain – shows the gathering of wild honey, and the earliest evidence of writing makes reference to the activity. Observations of honey's qualities and benefits as well as of bees were written by some of the earliest and most influential Greek and Roman philosophers, and, when the printing press was invented in Europe in the fifteenth century, treatises on beekeeping became, aside from the Bible, some of the most sought-after publications.

Honey in History

Along with being a source of food, energy and healing, honey seems to have played a significant role in economic and

Tetradrachm, about 390–300 BC, silver.

political history – there are even several instances in which it was used in warfare. Honey produced from the nectars of plants poisonous to humans was purposefully given to invading Greek soldiers in 401 BC in Trébizonde on the Black Sea in Turkey. In 67 BC Roman soldiers led by Pompey consumed the toxic substance, from which they quickly became sick and were then easily dispatched by their enemies, if they were not already dead from the lethal honey. (Bees were also used in warfare, but that is another story.)

Honey also figured significantly in trade and commerce. It was used extensively in many of the ancient cultures known to be involved in trade and assumptions can be made that it was a commodity as well. Egypt imported honey from surrounding lands during the time of the pharaohs, as early as 2500 BC. Beekeepers frequently carried their hives on barges up and down the Nile River, collecting nectar and selling honey along the way. Another region, the Indus Valley in Central Asia, was a centre of trade between 2000 and 1000 BC, and archaeological remains suggest that honey was a significant commodity. Similarly, Persia traded honey throughout its empire, which spread from the Nile to the Indus between 550 and 486 BC. The Greeks, Assyrians, Phoenicians, Romans and Arabs all traded honey, as did, to a lesser extent, the Chinese, along the Silk Road route that led to the Mediterranean from the second century BC to the fourteenth century AD In Central America, honey was apparently being traded by the Mayans during their heyday, from AD 250 to 900.

During the Middle Ages in Europe (approximately AD 500–1500), honey reigned as a sweetener, food, preservative and medicine, and as the basis of the ubiquitous alcoholic drink, mead. Beekeeping was a highly regarded skill, and was considered a necessity at every manor house and estate. In the tenth century, a Byzantine collection of writings on farming included sections on beekeeping.[13] Honey was often used as a form of currency, tribute or offering. In the eleventh century, for example, German peasants paid their feudal lords in honey and beeswax. Russia's forests held significant stores of wild honey, and this was harvested and traded throughout

Honeybee 'garden' of colourful wooden beehives in a village in Siberia, Russia.

the country as well as on the international honey route that included the Silk Road. Not only was honey valued, but so were other bee products, particularly wax from their hives, which was used to make candles. Bees also fascinated philosophers and theologians, who mused over the moral character of bees and the complex system of bee colonies.

Honey's importance in the West started to wane in the seventeenth century, when European countries were faced with political and social changes, industrialization and the rise in popularity and accessibility of sugar, which itself was tied to the spice and slave trades. The growth of cities and the shift from a rural to urban society meant the demise of beekeeping, so honey became less available, more expensive and increasingly a luxury item.[14] The Protestant Reformation also contributed to honey's decline, at least in Britain, when monasteries, which had historically been producers of honey, were closed in the 1530s.[15] In contrast, Spain and Portugal

Candle made of beeswax shaped like a skep, a traditional beehive made of straw.

Honey peddler in a market, San Antonio, Texas.

remained Catholic and kept their monasteries and convents, so honey continued to play a central role in their food – especially in their sweets and cakes. These, along with the honey itself, were often sold by the convents as a way to support the upkeep of the buildings, and were also shared with the public on feast days. Today *turron*, a taffy-like confection made of honey, is still an iconic sweet in Spain.

Sugar cane had been introduced into southern Europe by the Moors in the eighth century AD, but it did not overtake honey until that substance started to decline. Sugar's supremacy was encouraged later by the discovery of tea and spices in the 1400s, and the trade these engendered between Europe and the Orient (particularly China, India and Indonesia), which set the stage for later trade routes that formed between Africa and the European colonies for slaves, who were taken to settlements in the Caribbean such as the Hispaniola (now the Dominican Republic and Haiti) and Jamaica. There the slaves were traded for sugar to be sold in markets in Europe

(England, in particular) before the ships set sail for new supplies of slaves. This trade was driven partly by the discovery that sugar could provide a quick and inexpensive energy source for the masses of labourers working in the newly built factories in Europe and America, further enabling industrialization, urbanization and even the rise of capitalism.[16] By the mid-1800s, sugar had become cheaper than honey and had largely replaced it.

While honey continued to be a part of many culinary cultures, it did not play such a significant role. A luxury sweetener and comfort food rather than a necessity, it lost its place in medicine, health and other practical uses. It tended to be relegated to 'heritage food' or 'folk food' status, in that it was used by certain groups of people who lived in or maintained some cultural traditions outside of the mainstream. However, beekeeping itself often remained as a cottage industry and hobby, so honey was still produced, albeit on a small scale. There were always some aficionados of honey who kept up an interest in it: in 1874 an annual honey-judging competition that has continued to this day was first held at the Crystal Palace in London. Agricultural fairs typically include honey in their competitions, and the American Beekeeping Association holds an annual conference and trade show.

Honey is also now produced and distributed commercially on a larger scale and is added to a variety of products, particularly in industrialized nations.[17] It is sold in groceries and supermarkets, at farmers' markets, and on the Internet by beekeepers. It represents a significant economic contribution to small-scale producers as well as to several regions and nations. In 2010 alone 3–4 billion lb of honey was collected from 30 million bee colonies throughout the world.[18] These figures suggest that honey is certainly not disappearing from our cultural repertoire of foods. If anything, it is making a comeback.

2

Busy as a Bee: Honey Production and Harvesting

Bees are the true producers of honey; humans were simply fortunate enough to discover this natural source of energy and sweetness. They foraged for it in the wild, but also learned ways of 'managing' bees, so that they could have easier access to their honey and other products, particularly wax. These skills have been passed down over the centuries, and those who mastered them garnered respect and a secure place in society. Beekeeping has been an established occupation since the ancient Eqyptians, and continues into the present as both a profession and a hobby.

Honeybees: Life Cycle and Honey Production

Although there are more than 20,000 bee species, only a few of them can be domesticated. Primary among that small group is the honeybee. This species is not actually tamed, but their hives can be placed in locations useful and convenient for humans. In this way humans are able to control to some extent the flowering plants available for the bees as well as to collect the resulting honey more easily. According to

Wenceslaus Hollar, drawing of beekeeping in Roman times from Dryden's translation of Virgil's *Georgics* (1697).

Keith S. Delaplane, a professor and director of the Honeybee programme at the University of Georgia in the U.S., 'It is the dual assets of manageability and productivity that have secured for *Apis mellifera* its special place in human hearts and imagination, history and economy.'[1]

Common honeybees are highly social creatures with very organized, specific places in bee society. They are described as social because they cooperatively care for their brood, there is a division of labour in reproduction and generations co-exist.[2] Each group, called a colony, is ruled by a single queen, the only fertile female. She is tended by a small number of male drones, whose sole purpose in life seems to be to mate with her. The mating occurs in the air while in flight, and the act itself rips the sexual appendage from the drone, killing him. The queen mates with up to twenty drones over several days, then returns to the nest (or hive) to deposit the fertilized eggs into individual cells in the honeycomb. She stores the sperm and can lay nearly 1,500 eggs per day. It takes three days for an egg to hatch into a larva, which is tended to by younger, recently hatched adults who feed pollen to it. The larvae spend another eighteen days developing into the pupa stage and then adulthood.

The largest group of bees in a colony are the workers, which care for the eggs, feed the larvae until they hatch, guard the colony and clean the nest. They are the bees that fly out to gather nectar and pollen. They also guide the colony in decision-making activities through a remarkable behaviour called 'dancing', in which they communicate the direction, distance and quality of nectar and pollen sources, water or nesting sites. Worker bees live for only six weeks; drones for up to four months; and queens from two to three years.

Bees produce honey by carrying the nectar gathered from flowers back to their nest in a second stomach; at the nest

'Do you know how a bee makes honey?' cigarette card, early 20th century.

'The flies and the honey pot', cigarette card, early 20th century.

the other bees suck it out and chew it in order for enzymes to break it down into a simpler form of sugar. As mentioned previously, they then place it into cells of the comb and fan it with their wings to evaporate the water. At the same time, they add further enzymes. Once the honey is reduced to 18.6 per cent or less moisture content, the bees cap the honey with a thin cover of wax. Once it is capped, the honey is considered ripened, so beekeepers look for this white cover of wax before harvesting it from the hive. The average worker bee produces one-tenth to one-twelfth of a teaspoon of honey in its lifetime, and it is estimated that bees need to visit two million flowers in order to make 450 g (1 lb) of honey. One hive of bees typically needs 27–45 kg (60–100 lb) of honey to survive the winter in northern parts of the u.s. and Canada. It is easy to see how bees have acquired a reputation as constant and hard workers. It turns out, though, that bees are not really all that busy. Scientific observation and research has found that they spend only a few hours each day actually performing productive work.[5]

Harvesting Honey from the Wild

Honey was historically harvested from beehives in natural habitats, and still is in many places. This involves hunting for the nests and removing the comb that holds the honey. Bees often build their nests in out-of-the-way places such as sheer rock cliffs, tall trees and other sites where they are presumably safe from marauders, both animal and human.

Hunting for honey and gathering it was a dangerous task that required skill, courage, physical strength and agility, as well as the right equipment, such as a ladder made of vines or rope, a tool for cutting away some of the honeycomb and a vessel for carrying the honey. Another important requirement was an understanding of bees and knowledge about how to deal with their instinct to protect their nests by stinging. That information was usually carefully passed along within selected families or groups who specialized in honey hunting. Honey collecting, then, was a specialized, respected and valued activity – valued enough to warrant recording in even the earliest cultures.

The famous prehistoric cave painting of the 'Man of Bicorp' shows how difficult and dangerous honey hunting used to be. Found on the wall of the Spider Caves (Cuevas de la Araña) on the eastern coast of Spain, it shows two figures – men, presumably – climbing a long rope-like ladder that seems to be attached to the top of a cliff. The top figure is carrying a container and is poised next to a nest. He is

Wild beehive hanging from tree.

surrounded by bees (hopefully larger than life, since their size in the painting would equal that of a hawk today). The cave holding the painting is now part of a protected World Heritage Site, designated as rock art of the Iberian Mediterranean Basin, and in 1975 the image was reproduced on a stamp in Spain.

Such hunting and harvesting from the wild is still done today, usually using ancient techniques and skills that have been passed down in families and call for extensive apprenticeships. In northern India, for example, honey gatherers learn to follow bees into the forests and then climb trees to locate the hives hanging from the branches. In the Himalayan regions, bees build their nests in cliffs, which the honey hunters must scale to retrieve their prize. By tradition, the Gurung tribe in Nepal specializes in climbing down steep cliffs on rope ladders to reach the nests of giant honeybees, similar to the method shown in the paintings of the Spanish Spider Caves.

Gathering honey from giant Asian honeybees (*Apis dorsata*) calls for specialized skills, extensive knowledge of the bees themselves and a lot of courage. The stings of this type of bee can seriously injure and even kill humans. In the northern part of Malaysia, these bees construct gigantic honeycombs, as large as 2 m (6 ft) across, that hang from the native *tualang* trees, which can grow as high as 73 m (240 ft), and are the tallest tree so far discovered in Asia. Honey hunters there can be thought of as a clan – a family that not only inherited the skills and traditions for hunting honey, but had received legal permission to do so by the regional sultan. The bee scholar Stephen Buchmann visited the group, camping with them in the rainforest for a week while they prepared for the hunt by building ladders to attach to the tualang trees, along with other articles such as torches, cutting implements, buckets and a pulley system for lowering the honey-filled buckets. According to tradition, all of the tools had to be made from bone, wood or cowhide rather than metal. Secret rituals and prayers were conducted to ensure the safety of the men, and perhaps also to thank the bees. The actual hunting occurs at night, while the bees are sleeping. In a dangerous and arduous process, some of the men climb the trees – without light so as to not alarm the insects – to cut chunks of honeycomb that are then lowered to the ground in buckets. Torches on the ground create smoke to dull the bees' senses, while the sparks from the torches attract the bees, who follow the lights to the ground, where they remain until the sun comes up, when they find their way back up to their nests.[4]

Aboriginal Australians also have honey hunting traditions, although these peoples are in less danger from the activity since the bees found in such Australian regions are stingless. It takes great skill to find the nests, however, since the bees hide them high inside trees. Such honey trees are identified initially by listening at the trunk for the buzzing sound of the bees. Similarly, the Mayan peoples of the Yucatan Peninsula gathered honey from the native stingless bee (*Apidae meliponinae*). The bees build their nests in the wild in logs, and the Mayans learned how to replicate the logs with wooden hives. Some Mayan descendants still continue the tradition of gathering wild honey from logs in the tropical forests.[5]

One interesting aside in the history of gathering honey from the wild was the common belief that bees did not procreate but were somehow spawned from the heavens or, less prosaically, from the carcasses of animals. This belief continued well into the seventeenth century, and apparently even shows up in tales today. It also features in the Book of Judges in the Old Testament in a passage that recounts the story of Samson discovering honey in a dead animal:

And he turned aside to see the carcass of the lion and, behold, there was a swarm of bees and honey in the carcass. And he took thereof in his hands, and went on eating, and came to his father and mother, and he gave them, and they did eat but he told them not that he had taken the honey out of the carcass of the lion. (14:8–9)

Beekeeping

Bees cannot be domesticated in the usual sense of the word, but ancient peoples looked for ways of containing them so that their honey could be obtained more easily. Apiculture, the science and art of beekeeping, has a long history and involves the knowledge and skills of building and maintaining places for the bees to nest, how to care for the bees and how to extract the honey. It may have developed first in India and Egypt, although these may simply be the earliest-known cultures to have left some traces of the art. A leading authority on bees, Eva Crane, points out that many cultures simultaneously hunted honey in the wild and developed methods of beekeeping. Crane's influential history details those methods as they evolved throughout the world.[6]

Egyptian writings mention honey and bees as early as 3500 BC. Evidence of beekeeping from 2600 BC is found in a series of scenes on a relief in the Temple of the Sun in Egypt,

Sarawak: beehives hanging in a Sea Dayak's house, *c.* 1896.

which show men taking honey from one of nine hives, filling jars with the honey, pressing it, then sealing the jars. Hieroglyphic writing included with the images describes the scenes: 'bowling or smoking, filling, pressing, sealing of honey'.[7] The pharaoh apparently designated beekeepers with official titles – as 'Sealers of the Honey' – and they held a respected place in communities, but the art of beekeeping may have been practised at all levels of society. There is also evidence from the third century BC that hives were moved by beekeepers to catch the different flowerings – and flavours – in the same way they are today.

India used honey extensively and evidence shows that beekeeping appeared to develop there around 2000 BC. Sugarcane, however, displaced honey around AD 200, perhaps because of religious influences. Both Buddhism and Jainism, two of the major religions practised there, taught that their followers should not kill animals, nor deprive them of food and sustenance. Honey was food for the bees, so robbing the hives essentially depleted the insects' supplies, and honey gathering usually involved killing at least some of the bees that were protecting the home. Although legends say that the Buddha was nourished by honey brought to him by a monkey, strict adherents to those religions might not have considered honey a moral choice.[8]

A Hittite tablet dating from around 1300 BC stipulates a fine for stealing beehives, suggesting that beekeeping was well established in the Middle East in that era. Archaeological evidence from other early cultures in the Near East also demonstrates a tradition of beekeeping: clay and straw hives found in Israel date to 900 BC. The Hittites were probably a cultural link – in terms of beekeeping – between India (and Babylonia and Assyria) and Greece and Rome. Beekeeping was so important to the ancient Greeks that they even had a god of beekeeping, Aristaeus, and many famous philosophers, such as Aristotle, wrote about bees, as did the first-century BC poet Virgil and the first-century AD writer Pliny the Elder.[9] Virgil's poems portray bees as models for an orderly society, a theme frequently repeated throughout the world.

The Chinese developed beekeeping early on as well. The sixth-century BC scholar Fan Li wrote about the skills needed to manage bees and the importance of using wooden hives

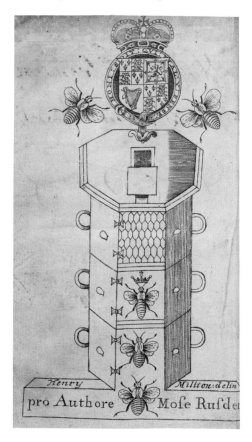

Skeps, woven cone-shaped beehives, as shown in this drawing from the 14th-century *Tacuinum sanitatis*, were typical of historical European beekeeping.

Medieval beehive with different types of bee.

in his *Golden Rules of Business Success*. Early Mayan cultures in Central America domesticated the stingless bees, *Melipona beecheii*, that were native to the region. Sixteenth-century accounts by Spanish explorers and colonizers observed and described methods of extracting the honey that did not destroy the hive. Logs were usually used as hives, simulating the wild colonies that thrived in the forests, and these were plugged with mud or a stone. Shed-like shelters were built around the log hives to protect them, most likely from natural predators.[10]

Beekeeping was practised across Europe, from the British Isles in the west through Eastern Europe and Russia. It was important enough that Welsh and Irish laws concerning the trade probably date to the sixth century. Those edicts specified how ownership of bee swarms would be determined, as well as proper restitution by the owner for injury or death from bee stings. Both cultures also have patron saints for beekeepers: St Gobnait (in English 'Deborah', which means honeybee) in Ireland; and the patron saint of Wales, St David, schooled the Welsh patron saint of bees, St Modomnoc of Ossory, who was actually Irish, and may have taken bees back to Ireland.

Other saints, too, have been designated by the Catholic Church as caretakers of bees as well as beekeepers. St Valentine is patron to beekeepers, along with young people, engaged couples and romantic love in general. St Ambrose, a fourth-century bishop of Milan and 'lover of virginity', is the patron saint of beekeepers, bees and candlemakers, among others, and is frequently pictured with bees or beehives. Legend tells of his father finding him with his face covered with bees as an infant, a sign that he would be 'honey-tongued' and eloquent in future. There is also the twelfth-century French monk St Bernard of Clairvaux, who became known as the 'mellifluous' or the 'honey-sweet doctor' because of his eloquence. His reputation may have come from his teaching that 'Jesus is honey in the mouth.' A critic

Headliner for *The American Bee Journal* (1881).

1. Dipping the Wooden Plate into melted Wax. 2. Peeling the Wax Sheet off the Wooden Plate. 3. Passing the Wax Sheet through the Foundation Machine. 4. A Sheet of Foundation fastened into a Frame, the Bees at work on it. 5. An American Apiary. 6. Uncapping the Cells. 7. Placing the Comb in the Extracting Machine. 8. Throwing the Honey out of the Comb. 9. Empty Comb ready to replace in the Hive, to be refilled with Honey by the Bees.
BEE KEEPING AND THE MANUFACTURE OF ARTIFICIAL HONEY-COMB.

Apiculture: scenes of bee-keeping and honey-gathering, 1885, wood engraving.

'W. J. Nolan, Agriculturist of the Bee Culture Laboratory at the National Agricultural Research Center [in Beltsville, Maryland] is demonstrating to Miss Lorry Van Houten how overcoats for bees protect these honey producers from the howling winds of winter', 11 April 1939.

of the over-indulgence of many in the church, he played a significant role in reforms as well as in later Christian mystical theology, somewhat fittingly for someone associated with the mysteries of bees and honey.[11]

That the Catholic Church recognized beekeeping is not surprising. The skill was practised and honed in monasteries throughout Christendom, partly because the beeswax from the honeycomb was so important for the provision of light using candles. Mead made from the honey provided sustenance and income to many monasteries, and some became renowned more for their mead than their piety. Monasteries were also the repositories of scholarly learning throughout the Middle Ages, and fostered education in Greek and Roman languages, thus keeping alive those ancient peoples' speculations about bees. These religious institutions produced their own treatises and manuals on beekeeping.

When the printing press was invented in the 1440s, beekeeping works were some of the first books printed, including the first-century Roman Columella's *De re rustica*. Another significant book was *A Further Discovery of Bees*, published in 1679 by Moses Rusden, the first Royal Bee Master appointed by Charles II. The 'common people', however, practised their own oral traditions and customs concerning bees and honey harvesting. By the 1800s publications on beekeeping were numerous, as were beekeeping associations and societies. In 1861 the *American Bee Journal* was established, and another journal, *Gleanings in Bee Culture*, began in 1873 in Medina, Ohio. Almost every country now has its own beekeeping associations, some of which are official governmental bodies – the U.S. Department of Agriculture, for example, establishes regulations and publishes pamphlets on the subject.

Beekeepers, meanwhile, in caring for their bees, frequently develop almost spiritual relationships with the insects. They learn how to move around the hives so as not to disturb the bees, and stories abound of beekeepers who are never stung by their bees. An American tradition that was probably brought from Europe claims that the bees must be told when their keeper dies, and that their hives should be draped in black. Otherwise, the bees will leave the hive in search of a new keeper. There have even appeared stories, including accounts reported in newspapers, of bees attending their keepers' funerals.

Beehives

A large amount of beekeeping history focuses on the designing of structures in which bee colonies can nest and build their combs. While man-made hives date back to the Egyptians, a major stride in European beekeeping was made in 1682 when an English clergyman, George Wheler, wrote about

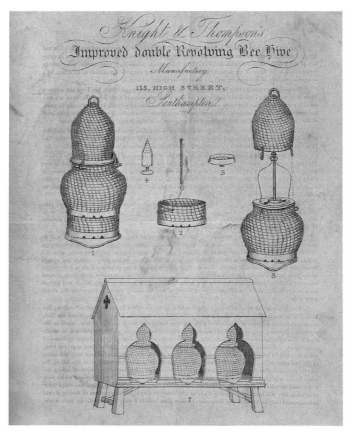

Apiculture: an advertising flyer for a patent beehive, after 1886, engraving after Knight and Thompson.

u.s. Department of Agriculture Agricultural Research Service scientists
Nathan Rice and Andy Ulsamer harvesting honey from the two colonies
at the People's Garden Apiary on the USDA Headquarters Whitten Building
roof, Washington, DC, 2014.

Greek hives. These creations were the forerunners of the movable frames commonly used by beekeepers today, and functioned so that the hive did not have to be destroyed – and the bees killed – in order to extract the honey. The modern beehive, as we know it today, was first designed in 1789 by the Swiss naturalist François Huber, who invented a wooden hive with a removable comb that could be taken out when full of honey and replaced with an empty one. In 1838 Huber's concept was refined by Johann Dzierzon in Poland.

The basic hive structure used by most contemporary bee-keepers was developed by the American Lorenzo Langstroth in 1860. He improved upon earlier designs by incorporating the concept of 'bee space', the gaps that bees create in their nests in order to be able to move around. The Langstroth hives involved reusable combs inserted into movable wooden frames that were then placed in boxes called 'supers'. These supers could be stacked on top of one another. Prior to the movable combs, honey production was limited to the amount of wax that the bees could make in a season. By lessening the work for the bees by contructing the combs for them, Langstroth improved the amount of honey that could be produced.

Beekeepers continue to experiment with hives, trying to find designs that better protect the bees and cause them less stress when their honey is harvested; on the other side of the beekeeping relationship, designs are also sought that make caring for bees and collecting honey easier and safer for humans.

Harvesting Honey from Kept Bees

The steps in harvesting honey made by 'kept' bees are basic-ally the same as they are when collecting honey from bees

Man holding a super, the removable part of a beehive that is taken out to drain the honey, *c.* 1940s.

in the wild. Smoke is used to calm the bees, allowing the beekeeper to remove the frames from the hive or honeycomb from the nest. With pre-built hives, bees are gently brushed from the frame, and the frames are placed in a box or taken away from the hive for harvesting. To extract the honey, the beeswax capping first has to be removed – either by hand with a knife or with an electric knife. The frames can be stood in containers to catch the dripping honey, but are most commonly placed into a hand-cranked or electric centrifuge that spins the comb around, forcing the honey to pour out. The frames and wax comb can then be placed back into the hive for the bees to repeat the process and again begin to line them with honey. Since removing frames takes a certain amount of strength and can potentially harm the bees (and the beekeeper, too), new hive designs try to remedy these problems. A structure has been developed in Australia, for

Esan Safieh, the Bethlehem Poultry Farm, showing a honeycomb lifted from the hive.

Honey extractor machine.

example, that does not call for movable frames – instead, the honey flows out of the hive via tubes.

Once removed from the hive, the honey can be put straight into jars and containers, but more commonly it is filtered to remove larvae, bits of honeycomb, dead bees, twigs and other surplus material. The fineness of the filtering varies, with the most sophisticated processing removing bee pollen and propolis as well. Some producers slowly heat the honey in order to destroy crystals, but this has to be done gradually and cautiously, and most small-scale producers do not use heat at all. (A notable harvesting trick is knowing that the honey needs to be warm in order to spin out of the centrifuge and flow.)

Beehives in a small town in Washington State.

Some honey producers also harvest the comb, which is usually placed in a jar topped off with liquid honey, although some beekeepers sell blocks of the honeycomb. In order to create comb honey, beekeepers use special supers designed to encourage the bees to make more comb (called 'drawing').

The Honey Industry

Honey is produced both as a home-based cottage industry and by larger commercial producers. The latter are defined as those with 300 or more hives, and beekeeping associations try to maintain standards for sustainable production. The National Honey Board estimated that there were 115,000 to 125,000 beekeepers in the United States in 2012.[12] About 1,200 of those are migratory beekeepers who move their bees around the country to pollinate crops, particularly almonds and blueberries, which are dependent on pollination by bees.

China is the world's largest exporter of honey, and the u.s. is both a large importer and exporter. Managed honeybees from beekeepers with five or more colonies in the u.s. produced 80 million kg (178 million lb) of honey in 2014.[13] Besides China and the u.s., the other main producers of honey today include Argentina and Turkey.

In the first decade of the twenty-first century, beekeepers in the u.s. dealt with numerous problems affecting the health of their bees: varroa mites, which attack and kill bees; Colony Collapse Disorder (ccd), the mysterious destruction of entire colonies; and pesticides and insecticides that have the unintended but unfortunate result of poisoning bees or wiping out their habitats. Contemporary standards of beauty for gardens, parks and public spaces – as well as for recreational land, such as golf courses – have no use for numerous plants that are in fact beneficial for bees. Dandelions, for example, are excellent sources of nutrients for bees, but are considered weeds by many people and frequently controlled, that is, eradicated.

These losses of healthy bee colonies have significantly affected both large- and small-scale beekeeping operations. When producers are unable to gather enough honey to sell it at a profit, the market price is inevitably raised, but many consumers seem to consider honey a luxury and are either unwilling or unable to pay the higher prices. Honey is sometimes diluted with corn syrup or other ingredients in order to be sold for less, but this undermines the local industries (not to mention destroying the quality and taste of the honey). Also, in the u.s. imported honey is frequently less expensive than that which is locally produced; however, it is not so heavily regulated, so customers may be purchasing diluted products. These cheap imports are having a negative impact on domestic producers, threatening the sustainability of the

American honeybee industry.[14] Not all imports are diluted or inexpensive, but pure honeys tend to be found in speciality or ethnic markets: for example, buckwheat honey from Eastern Europe, a number of Greek honeys or some New Zealand varieties. Undiluted, locally produced honey is now found mainly in health food chains, farmers' markets and high-end food shops.

The concerns over the health of bees and the price of honey are spreading around the globe. Perhaps as consumers become more aware of the benefits, both to themselves and to nature, of high-quality honey (in terms of health and taste) and begin to recognize the rich heritage represented in each sweet drop, they will be willing to pay more for it and be disposed to take precautions to protect the bees and their habitats.

3
Main Course and Dessert: Honey as Food

Honey is one of the oldest foods in the world. Although its nutritional content is primarily sugar (fructose and glucose), and it is 17 to 19 per cent water, it also contains antioxidant vitamins, minerals and enzymes. At approximately 64 calories per tablespoon, it offers energy along with a mouthful of sweetness that is both intense and flavourful. Not only can the sweet, syrupy liquid be eaten as a meal in itself, but it can be added as a sweetener to foods and drinks, or used as an ingredient in preparing other foods. Sometimes it acts as a binder to hold other ingredients together or is used as a preservative. The honey itself carries with it other bee-produced products that are sometimes eaten with it or as separate foods: the wax honeycomb that the bees make to hold their offspring; the larvae themselves; propolis, the glue-type substance the bees make from plant resin; bee pollen (the pellets of pollen that they use to feed themselves rather than turn into honey); and royal jelly, the special food for the babies that have been selected as potential queen bees. Other than the combs and larvae, these products can be gathered by humans, though in quantities too small to be consumed as a meal, but they may instead be used as nutritional supplements. All of them, though, are naturally found in honey and so will be consumed,

Bees and a traditional straw skep (beehive) decorate this tin of honey.

sometimes intentionally, sometimes not. Honey and these various products show up in everyday consumption and in symbolic meals and rituals throughout history in various parts of the world.

Honey is now available in various forms and qualities, and is regulated by trade and health associations. It is generally considered natural and healthy, even a comfort food, although somewhat expensive compared to sugar. It also seems to be a universal food, with only a few ethical or religious prohibitions arising against its consumption from strict vegans, some followers of Buddhism and most Jains.

The flavours of honey are as numerous as the varieties of flowering plants available, reflecting the plants whose nectars were gathered by the bees, which, in turn, reflect the different geographic regions of the globe. In this way, honey offers a very sweet and concentrated example of *terroir*, the French concept of 'taste of place'. The soil, climate and surrounding species of flora and fauna affect the plants and their nectars, thus affecting the taste, contents and quality of the honey. Consuming honey, then, connects us – physically and literally – to nature and specific spaces and cultures.

Honey in the Ancient World

We can assume that early humankind consumed honey whenever and wherever it was found, which would have originally been Central, South and Southeast Asia, and later the east coast of Spain, other Mediterranean regions, Central and Southern Africa and Central America.

Ancient cultures as well as contemporary hunter-gatherers – and plenty of modern aficionados of raw honey – treated the wax honeycomb as a meal in itself, frequently consuming the other substances, such as the larvae, propolis, bee pollen, royal jelly and any dead bees or twigs, caught in the sticky 'liquid gold'. A number of references to honeycomb in mythology and scriptures suggest its importance in early diets. In India, between the sixth and fourth centuries BC, a monkey brought honeycomb to the Buddha when he broke his fast after achieving enlightenment, even picking out the larvae so that it would be fit for a vegetarian. Similarly, according to the biblical record, in AD 33 Jesus was offered honeycomb by his disciples when he reappeared after his crucifixion. Alexander the Great, during his attempt to capture Central Asia in the years between 331 and 327 BC, praised the wild honeycombs of the Caspian Mountains. Obviously, honeycomb was considered edible and healthful as well as a tasty treat.

From ancient times, honey was also an important ingredient in food preparation. Early written documents from ancient Egypt, Pompeii, Sumer, Babylon, Greece and Rome even give a few recipes. It was a common sweetener for the grain porridge that was the standard meal consumed by the masses in these cultures, but those with wealth or royalty used it in more elaborate ways. Archaeologists discovered residues of a 2,700-year-old caramelized honey and fennel tart along with mead buried with King Midas in western Turkey.[1]

Wealthy Egyptians used honey to make a wheat flour bread that was 'sculpted into animal, bird, or insect shapes before it was baked'.[2] The Greeks used their renowned honey from Mount Hymettus to flavour wine, porridge, fish and salads. Roman banquets included honey and vinegar sauces on their meats and vegetables, and topped their cheese and cheesecakes with honey; they even made honey omelettes, and consumed a wine and honey drink. A number of recipes using honey were recorded in around the fourth century AD in the cookbook *De re coquinaria*, attributed to Marcus Gavius Apicius, a culinary expert and advisor to the emperors Tiberius and Augustus in the first century AD.

Cakes made of honey (almost equal parts honey and flour) figured significantly in both commonplace and ritual use among both the Greeks and the Romans, and these were often moulded into a variety of shapes appropriate for the occasion. They were used as offerings to the gods, as amulets for protection, tokens of affection and souvenirs. Honey cakes made of wheat flour, honey and sesame seeds were shaped into male and female genitalia as offerings to the Greek goddess of agriculture and fertility, Demeter.[3]

Other parts of the world used honey in their culinary traditions as well, but recorded recipes are lacking. We can assume honey was eaten in early India since the Buddha is said to have eaten a honey ball for strength during his search for enlightenment. Honey was probably an ingredient throughout the Indian subcontinent for flatbreads and fried dough balls; it would have been drizzled on top, helping herbs or seeds, such as sesame seeds, adhere to the bread. It is likely that this is the origin of *gulab jamun*, a fried dough ball of milk, flour, butter, oil, cardamom, sugar or honey that is then soaked in a sweet syrup flavoured with saffron, rosewater and cardamom, which is found throughout the region. Indians and Central Asians probably mixed honey in with yoghurt, as did the Greeks, and may have used it to sweeten their yoghurt-based drinks, *lassis*, that are still found in the area today.

In China, honey was used as a seasoning at least as early as the Han dynasty (200 BC to AD 220) and sweetened ginger tea. Although Chinese cuisine did not feature honey, Li Po, a poet of the Tang Dynasty in the eighth century AD, praised its varieties and abundance. Central Asia most likely had its own culinary traditions surrounding honey since honeybees

Fragment from a jar with a label identifying the contents as honey, Egypt, *c.* 1390–1352 BC.

Indian sweet soaked in honey.

thrived in that region. The cultural interchanges occurring historically throughout Central Asia, the Mediterranean and the Middle East are represented today by ubiquitous honey-laden pastries, such as *baklava*.

Arabian and North African cultures used honey as a sweetener, particularly on porridges made of semolina. Dates also provided sugar and appeared to grow more easily, so those seem to have surpassed honey as the sweetener of choice – whether by necessity or due to availability or expense. The ancient Hebrews, however, frequently referred in their scriptures to the sweetness of honey, suggesting that it was a familiar and desirable substance.

Central American cultures – Mayan, Inca, Olmec, Mixtec, Toltec and Aztec – used native honey as a sweetener for corn-based breads and drinks, perhaps as early as 9,000 years ago. The honey would have been harvested from wild indigenous stingless bees that built nests in the forests, but beekeeping was

Kubo Shunman (1757–1820), *Hives with Wasps, and a Box with a Spoon for Honey*, print.

also practised. When European explorers came to the region in the 1500s, they were astonished to find well-developed systems of beehives. The bees themselves were probably also eaten, and the honey used to flavour other native foods, such as the trinity of beans, corn and squash as well as meats and chilli peppers. Honey-roasted squash is a traditional dessert dish today in Mexico, and probably originated in earlier times.

Honey in European Cultures

Early central, northern and western Europeans consumed honey, both wild and 'kept'. The British Isles had an early tradition of a honey cuisine. The Druids, a pre-Christian religious group among the Celts of Ireland, Britain and Gaul (France), called Britain 'Honey Isle', suggesting the prevalence of bees and honey there.[4] England later became renowned for its thyme honey and Scotland for heather honey, and monasteries raised bees for their honey and beeswax. Wales and Ireland both have legends associating bees and honey with their patron saints: an angel appeared to the father of St David of Wales, claiming that he would have a son in thirty years who would be known for 'honeyed wisdom', as symbolized by a honeycomb. David did indeed establish monasteries with bee colonies throughout the country. While monasteries seem to have been most interested in honey as an ingredient in mead, it was also given to the poor and was probably used as a medicine, health tonic and preservative as well as a sweetener and food. (They also used the beeswax for candles.)

Legends also explain why bees thrived in Ireland but not in Wales. One of St David's monks in Wales, St Domnoc (or Modomnoc), tried three times to cross the channel to Ireland, but bees followed him, settling on his boat. He went back to Wales to return the bees, but they refused to leave him. St David then gave his blessing to Domnoc, who was followed by the bees to Ireland, where he established a monastery. The bees thrived there, and honey became an established part of the region's culinary traditions.

Early Slavic, Scandinavian and Germanic peoples were known to keep bees, and both ate the honey and used it to either sweeten other brewed beverages or to make mead. These were then considered foods, not just refreshing drinks, and their appearance in legends and myths suggest that they were a significant part of the foodways of the people. Like the Greeks, the ancient Germanic tribes mixed honey with milk and melted butter to create a nutritious food for children.[5]

Europeans during the Middle Ages were more likely to turn honey into mead than to eat it, but it was still used in breads (cakes, biscuits, flatbreads and pancakes) and sauces for sweet and savoury foods. The sauces may have helped to disguise the 'off' tastes of older meat, but they also added moisture, flavour and even health benefits. As Bee Wilson, an authority on the subject, explains: 'Honey was more than just a sweetener in pre-sugar times. It was highly valued as an ingredient which could restore harmony to a dish, correcting faults in other components of the meal.'[6] It may also have been used as a glaze to give a golden tint to foods, since colourful foods were considered more desirable.

Honey cakes were baked from whatever grains were available – generally wheat, rye and oats. These cakes frequently included spices, so were sometimes known as spice cakes or gingerbread. As in early Greece and Italy in the Middle Ages, this malleable food was often pressed into moulds that gave the cakes designs and shapes. They were given as tokens of affection and souvenirs and were common fare for times of celebration. German *Lebkuchen* (a gingerbread-like baked good), for example, were – and still are – shaped into pigs for New Year's festivities. Honey was also used as syrup and drizzled on porridge (the medieval dish frumenty) and breads, particularly the pancake-like flatbreads cooked on griddles that were a standard food item for the common people.

Honey was frequently used to preserve meat, fruit and eggs. Those foods would be packed in honey, and the honey was then eaten with that item — or used in its preparation. This may be the root of the culinary tradition of including

Spice cookies made of honey, purchased from a Ukrainian grocery store in Parma, Ohio.

sweet-flavoured foods and ingredients in some savoury dishes, such as meat and vegetables stewed in honey and water. The traditional Eastern European meat and vegetable stew *tzimmes* could be a holdover from that era.

Sugar started replacing honey as the sweetener, medicine and preservative of choice in Western Europe around the 1600s. It was less expensive, which was tied directly to the new trade routes established at sea that connected sugar, spices and the slave trade. Honeybees, however, were still taken to the colonies being established by the Spanish, Portuguese, Dutch, British and other European powers. In the New World of North America, honey had to vie with other sweeteners, such as maple syrup, molasses and sorghum, as well as sugar, that were becoming increasing popular. Australia acquired beekeeping and honey in the 1800s following settlement of the land by the British, and the country soon became a major honey producer and consumer.

The Twenty-first Century

Today, honey is available throughout the world and seems to have some place, however small, in every food culture. It shows up as a sweetener to add to food or drinks; as an ingredient in desserts or sweet snacks; in glazes, sauces, dips and condiments for meats and vegetables; and as a spread or syrup on breads and cakes. It is stirred into butter, cheeses and yoghurts, and it flavours sweet foods, cereals, baked goods and medicines, particularly throat lozenges.

It also appears in a number of ritual and festive dishes, particularly from culinary cultures stemming from the Middle East, Eastern Europe and Central Asia, where it frequently symbolizes the sweetness of life or hopes for the New Year. Jewish tradition, for example, includes a honey cake at Rosh Hashanah (New Year) as well as a symbolic dish of honey, walnuts and apples during Passover. (Moreover, in Jewish tradition in medieval Europe, children had their alphabet tablets smeared with honey to symbolize the sweetness of learning.) The Persian New Year is similarly celebrated with a honey cake. Buddhist practices include a honey-offering ritual, and numerous cultures feature honey in traditional recipes for special sweets, such as the Central American fried pastry *sopaipillas*, Mediterranean and Middle Eastern *baklava*, and Eastern European honey cakes and biscuits. The relative expense of honey compared with sugar makes these treats even more special and celebratory.

Many honey aficionados insist that honey is best eaten raw and that cooking destroys its flavour, texture and nutritional

Boxes of honey-flavoured cereal show how honey is used to suggest a healthy and nutritious food.

benefits. The food writer Bee Wilson, for example, states: 'If you have some wonderful honey, the best thing you can do is to eat it in its unadulterated state, perhaps with yoghurt or good bread . . . Do not use your very finest honeys for cooking. They would be wasted.'[7] Part of honey's appeal, though, is that it can be enjoyed in a variety of states, including uncooked or simply licked off whatever implement is used to remove it from a hive or container, whether that is a spoon, a twig or one's own fingers. A snack that is now available is a honey 'stick', a narrow, plastic honey-filled tube about the size of a straw. One end can be torn (or bitten or cut) off, and the honey is squeezed out. Popular for sampling honey

'Cool Honey' Altoids.

varieties, honey sticks also make the sticky liquid an easy on-the-go snack. Flavourings are added to the honey, so the sticks are usually available in a number of popular flavours that one might not normally consider: cinnamon, pink lemonade, chocolate and caramel, to name a few.

Honeycomb can also be eaten along with the honey, and is consumed particularly by beekeepers and those who are familiar with the older ways of preserving and selling honey with the honeycomb intact. A few cultural groups, ranging from peoples of the Himalayas to those of Borneo, Yemen, Australia and Central Africa, still make honeycomb into a meal.[8] As recently as the 1950s, the Mbuti people of Central Africa, for example, depended on wild honeycomb for 70 per cent of their diet, eating as much as 900 g (2 lb) a day.[9]

Honey today is frequently more expensive than sugar and other common sweeteners, particularly artificial ones or those made from the ubiquitous darling of the industrialized food system, high-fructose corn syrup. Although its status as a food has declined across much of the world, honey is still

Baklava in Tel Aviv.

purposefully used in different ways and for a multiplicity of reasons, including its recognition as a culturally important foodstuff in many culinary traditions; its historical continuity with past recipes; its significance in celebratory feasts; its value to people on a personal level; and its use by health-conscious individuals as a modern lifestyle choice. Personal taste, of course, comes into play, and those who appreciate the flavours of real honey varieties tend to value it highly.

The Morality and Ethics of Honey as Food

Honey is frequently offered as a more natural and more sustainable sweetener than cane or beet sugar. Sugar cane's history is tied to colonialism and the slave trade, and it is now highly processed and firmly part of the industrial and capitalist food system. Honey, meanwhile, has retained its associations with the natural world, and although there are companies producing and selling it on a large scale – especially to mainstream supermarkets – it is also widely available from small-scale beekeepers and at farmers' markets. Purchasing it, then, can be viewed as a political or ethical statement, and it is often associated with 'alternative lifestyle' diets, such as vegetarianism and veganism. However, honey is an animal by-product, and some bees, as mentioned previously, are usually killed in the process of the honey being taken from their hive. There is debate, therefore, within the vegan community over the ethics of consuming honey, and many vegans choose not to do so, since they consider it against the tenets of veganism, 'which excludes all forms of exploitation, and cruelty to, the animal kingdom'.[10]

Jainism, founded in the sixth century BC in India, similarly forbids the killing of any living animal, so the ingestion of honey is prohibited. Buddhism, which also originated in India during the same period, has similar proscriptions against killing animals and states that killing bees generates bad karma. Nevertheless, honey retains an important place as a healthy and auspicious food, as well as a medicine, and the phrase 'honey-tongued' was used by the Buddha to refer to honest and pleasant speech. Within Judaism and Islam, honey is considered kosher and halal respectively, meaning proper to eat, even though the bee itself is considered unclean.

Flavours of Honey

Both the flavour and colour of honey depend on the nectars collected. Monofloral or varietal honeys come from a single type of plant, although they might contain traces of other nectars, while multifloral honeys come from multiple plants. Bees travel up to 5 km (3 miles), although some say 8 km (5 miles), from their hive, so beekeepers place the hives within 1 and 1.5 km (½ and 1 mile) of the plants whose nectar is desired. Both monofloral and multifloral honey are identified by the plants producing the nectar. Also, some regions are associated with specific plants and therefore specific types of honeys, and those place names are frequently given to the resulting honeys as well. Many books on honey list the most famous places, plants and their associated honeys. Hattie Ellis offers descriptions of ninety varieties by plant source in a chapter of her book on honey titled 'Around the World in 90 Pots'.[11]

Among the most famous of the speciality flavours and varieties of honey associated with place are Greek thyme and Greek mountainside, the latter including marjoram, thyme and other herbs; Scottish heather; Florida tupelo; southern Appalachian sourwood: New Zealand manuka, tawari or beechwood; Australian eucalyptus, blue gum or chia; Italian or Spanish chestnut; Arbutus, also called strawberry tree, from Sardinia and Portugal (also called *corbezzolo* honey or bitter honey in Italy); Hungarian, Bulgarian and Romanian acacia, also known as black locust in the southeastern u.s.; Central European buckwheat; Brazilian Christmas berry; Ethiopian coffee; Russian clover; Himalayan balsam and so on. Particular countries and regions are famous for their variety of honey, including Germany, Eastern Europe and Russia, Cyprus, Minorca, Scotland and Greece.

Honey flavours obviously speak of place, but some plants, such as clover and alfalfa, are now raised wherever there is industrial agriculture, so modern honey is losing some of its *terroir*. Commercial honey is now frequently made up of blends, producing a generic and standardized flavour.

Quality of Honey

The Roman poet Ovid believed that the quality of honey depends on the 'nobility of the carcase that produced the

Jar of 'summer thistle' honey home-produced in southern Appalachia, and of local wildflower honey.

bees'.[12] Most beekeepers now acknowledge that it depends chiefly upon the quality of the nectars collected by the bees, contrary to the nineteenth-century American poet Emily Dickinson's claim that

> The pedigree of honey,
> Does not concern the bee;
> A clover, any time, to him
> Is aristocracy.[13]

The quality of honey is not regulated by official government organizations, but suggested guidelines do exist. The National Honey Board, which proclaims honey 'one ingredient: the way nature intended', offers ways of evaluating the quality, texture, colour, content, flavour and source of the over 300 varieties of honey found in the u.s. It identifies colour as ranging from light to dark (with the darker having more health benefits and stronger flavours), offers descriptions of flavours and suggests that the best way to taste honey is to let a spoonful melt in one's mouth, allowing it to slowly spread across the tongue. The u.s. Department of Agriculture (USDA) also offers 'standards' of honey, which are used in labelling honey that is commercially distributed. It recognizes two types of honey: filtered, in which all or most other substances found in raw honey have been removed, and strained, in which grains of pollen, small air bubbles and very fine particles are not filtered out. The USDA then issues grades based on moisture content, absence of defects, flavour and aroma, and clarity. Grade A is the highest quality and C is the lowest.[14] The European Union safeguards the naming of honeys, and its system certifies different types – thus protecting food products from imitations and false advertising – based on Protected Geographical Indication (PGI) and Protected Designations of Origins (PDO). Individual countries also give their stamp of approval.

After honey has been gathered from the bees, it is processed and packaged in a variety of ways. These are identified with specific terms used by the honey industry that are frequently placed on labels and in marketing descriptions. 'Liquid honey', for example, which is the most common form of modern honey, is honey in its natural form, although it is a thicker and more viscous substance than a typical fluid. It is usually presented in glass jars, covered ceramic bowls or plastic containers (the latter sometimes in the shape of a bear). Honey in this form can be easily poured or spooned, but tends to be too runny and sticky to be neatly removed from a container and transported to another dish or food (or one's mouth). Special honey dippers – sticks with ridges on one end – make it easier to work.

Jar of 'raw' honey with honeycomb.

'Comb' honey, or honeycomb, is also in its natural form, but is either attached to the beeswax or is packaged unfiltered, still containing bits of the comb. Some people enjoy chewing on the wax, but it is not normally ingested. Although the comb does not seem to add to the taste of the honey, it does give it an aura of naturalness. Historically, it was probably eaten, along with any bee larvae and other bee products, as is still regularly practised by some cultures. 'Set', 'creamed' or 'whipped' honey is the most convenient and least messy form of honey. A small amount of 'seed honey' – crystallized honey – is mixed into liquid honey, making it less runny and giving it a creamy texture. It also changes colour slightly, turning opaque rather than clear and golden. Whipped honey is frequently offered as a sweet topping to spread on bread or other baked goods, and it works well in sandwiches since, unlike liquid honey, it does not seep through the bread.

Another set of descriptors used in packaging honey refers to how it has been processed once it is out of the hive. The 'filtered' and 'strained' designations mentioned above do not change the actual honey, but heat does, so it is important to identify if heat has been applied. The normal temperature of a hive is about 35°C (95°F). Higher temperatures make the honey flow out more easily and kill potential bacteria, but they also destroy some of the honey's health benefits. Raw honey is honey that has neither been heated beyond the normal hive temperature nor been put through a fine filter or strainer, so it contains some pollen and usually some wax. Although it is said to have more health benefits than the heated alternative, processed honey, it crystallizes more quickly, and is sometimes perceived by those uneducated in honey matters as having gone bad. Raw honey also tends to be very runny, making it good for stirring into drinks and food, but its sticky factor makes it a problem for some consumers who dislike the texture or find it inconvenient. Unpasteurized honey is the same as raw honey; pasteurized honey, on the other hand, is honey that has been heated – officially in order to kill any yeast cells that might cause fermentation. Ideally, it is heated quickly and only to 71°C (160°F), but producers differ in their methods. The word 'pasteurized', however, tends to carry connotations of cleanliness and safety for mainstream consumers, and creates an assumption of better quality and security.

Honey can be eaten by itself or mixed with other ingredients. Natural or pure honey has had no additives, preservatives or synthetic ingredients added. Also referred to as 'undiluted', it is usually more expensive than diluted honeys. Natural honey can also be called 'blended honey', in which honeys from various sources are blended together – not by the bees, but by human processors and distributors in stages after the honey has been collected. Blending is frequently done for taste as well as marketing reasons, especially since some consumers find the darker honeys too strong. Mixing different types of honey together can make it more palatable, and also gives a more uniform flavour – this is an important consideration for producers and retailers, who feel the need to guarantee reliable, unsurprising (typically mild) flavours to their customers. Clover is one of the most popular honeys in the u.s., and its mild flavour and taste have become familiar to many Americans. Some varieties of *Verbena cloverae* are native to North America, but others have been imported and have thrived, so that clover is now the most common flower used for commercial honey production. Clover honey distributed commercially is usually blended from a variety of clovers — alsike, red, yellow and white — found in different regions in order to achieve a standard flavour.

A final category found in honey marketing is 'organic', a somewhat confusing nomenclature to consumers since it would seem that all honey comes from bees and is therefore undoubtedly organic. In this context, though, the term refers to honey produced from the nectars of plants that have not been exposed to pesticides or herbicides. Some organic honeys also specify that they are non-GMO, meaning that the plant sources for the nectar have not been genetically modified. These honeys tend to be more expensive than others and somewhat controversial (particularly by those who claim that the quality and benefits of the honey are actually negatively impacted by those substances). Also, the subject of genetically modified organisms (GMOs) is itself controversial in the u.s., and not all consumers and scientists agree that such products generate harmful effects. The European Union, however, has banned the use of GMOs and heavily regulated the importation

Russian children eating honey fresh from the hive, early 20th century.

of foods containing them. Be that as it may, organic honey is frequently preferred by consumers concerned with the effects of modern industrial agriculture on the environment and human health, and can be found in some mainstream super-markets as well as health food stores or farmers' markets.

4

The Nectar of the Gods: Honey as Drink

Honey has been consumed in liquid form for at least as long as it has been eaten as a food. Its use in this way is perhaps even more widespread, since it has often been used to sweeten other drinks, ranging from more innocent beverages such as tea, lemonade or chocolate to tonics of vinegar, water and alcoholic libations – wine, ale, beers, whisky and more. Left to itself, honey with a little bit of added water naturally ferments into mead, probably the oldest alcoholic beverage known to humankind, but it can also ferment when mixed with other substances. The nomenclature for this variety of drink is confusing, because the name 'mead' is often used interchangeably with 'honey wine', as well as others, depending on the culture and era. Also, it is not always clear from the historical records whether or not the drinks were fermented. Honey-based drinks, in general, have been used throughout history for medicine, celebrations, ceremonies and religious rituals, as well as for refreshment, nourishment and to add flavour to a meal. Mead in particular plays a large role in mythology, folklore and history, and is enjoying a popularity today that is reviving many older recipes and creating a renewed appreciation for honey.

Non-alcoholic Drinks with Honey

Perhaps the simplest drink of all, which was possibly even consumed by the ancient Greeks, is honey stirred into water, with or without the comb. The fourth-century AD Roman scholar Rutilius Taurus Aemilianus Palladius described four kinds of honey drinks: *hydromel* (honey and water), *rhodomel* (with rose petals), *omphacomel* (fruit juice and honey) and *oenomel* (honey, water and grape must).[1] These could be drunk freshly made, but were probably also left to ferment.

As a sweetener, honey is today most commonly added to tea, a practice recorded in China as early as the Han Dynasty (206 BC–AD 220). Drinks made from sour fruits, such as lemon, lime or tamarind, were also historically sweetened with honey, and now tend to be considered healthier than those using cane or beet sugar, because of the type of sugar making up honey.

This addition of honey to drinks has a long history as a restorative and curative tonic. Until very recently, when the medical establishment decided that it was unsafe, honey was considered healthy for infants and was frequently mixed into warm milk as a nutritious and comforting food. Hot tea with lemon and honey is nowadays frequently taken as a home remedy to soothe a sore throat or cough. Similarly, a Dutch beverage called *kwast,* made of hot water, lemon and honey and sometimes enhanced with alcohol, is used to fend off colds and chest ailments. A traditional drink in southern Appalachia is 'switchell', a mixture of water, vinegar and honey that was habitually used as both a tonic and a simple, refreshing drink.

Honey Added to Alcoholic Beverages

The variety of alcoholic drinks involving honey is confused by terminology. Mead technically refers to fermented honey and water, but can also include a grain in the fermenting process. In other cases, the honey is added after the fermentation has occurred, in a process that distinguishs mead from wine, beer and distilled spirits.

Wine is made from fermented grapes or other fruits. It is unclear in some of the ancient literature as to whether honey would have been added during the wine's creation or afterwards, but adding honey to wine seems to have been customary wherever wine was made. The Greeks and Romans certainly did so. In Homer's *Odyssey*, 'honey-heartened wine' was used to ritually close a feast and was also offered to the gods for protection. By the first century BC lots of varieties of wine were known. The Romans made an inexpensive alcoholic drink called *mulsum*, which was honey mixed with water and wine, and 'was so inexpensive to make that the government doled it out to the common people to fire up their patriotism during public events'.[2] It was so popular in the first century AD that it increased the demand for honey throughout the empire.

Beer, meanwhile, differs from wine in that it is derived from fermented grains to which yeast is added. It can also be as simple as yeast bread left to ferment in water, although such crude beer was historically imbibed only by the peasant classes. Because of its basis in grain, beer throughout history and across much of the world was considered a food. Honey was usually added after the beverage had finished fermenting in order to give it a sweetness and to add flavour. The current trend in home brewing and speciality beers includes experimenting with honey and highlighting the floral quality that the honey lends to the beer.

In Scotland, honey was traditionally used in distilling malt whisky. Today, Drambuie is the brand name for a liqueur of malt whisky, heather honey, herbs and spices that dates at least to 1745. Numerous other similar drinks have been created, both historically and in the present day, ranging from a version of Jack Daniel's Tennessee Whiskey, a Polish honey vodka, a honey-infused grappa from Italy, and honey- and chai-flavoured beer brewed in Ohio. There are many varieties of alcoholic drinks featuring honey in some way: from fruity punches to Martinis, milk-based cocktails and the popular American party drink 'Jello shots'.[3] Mead can also be made into honey jack, similar to applejack, through freeze distillation, in which a portion of mead is frozen and then the ice removed.

Honey Wine

Drinks called honey wine are technically a mixture of fermented honey, water and grapes, but they also refer to fermented honey and water, that is, mead. The word 'wine' is perhaps used in place of 'mead' since it suggests more refinement, but it creates a great deal of confusion. Melomels, on the other hand, are meads fermented with fruits other than grapes, so are not true wines. One type of melomel made with grape juice, however, is *pyment*, but it is not considered a wine since the skins of the grapes are not used.

Perhaps the most famous honey wine is *tej*, the national drink of Eritrea and Ethiopia. It is flavoured with a type of hops called *gesho*, and always referred to as a wine. It is said that King Solomon and the Queen of Sheba toasted each other with *tej*.

Mead

Mead, derived from the old English 'meodu', is made by fermenting honey and water or by fermenting honey, water and a grain. It occurs naturally whenever honey and water are left to sit for an extended time, since wild yeasts float in the air and will settle in the liquid, causing it to ferment. Mead was therefore probably the first alcoholic drink ever created. It would have been a case of humankind stumbling across it by accident, appreciating its taste and then purposely setting out to make it. The influential anthropologist Claude Lévi-Strauss believed that mead represented a transition between nature and

Bottle of Lindisfarne mead.

culture. In one of his seminal studies on the development of culture, *Du miel aux cendres* (From Honey to Ashes), published in 1960, he recounts a legend from the Chaco people of the Amazon in which mead was 'discovered' by an old man who accidentally left honey and water together that then fermented.

The naturalness of mead is one reason it was so prevalent historically. The fermentation process usually took a fairly long time, however, since honey lacks the acids and tannins needed for the yeast to survive. To make up for that, a grain, particularly hops, was frequently added, aiding in both the fermentation process and in preservation. Fruit juices also added some of the needed acids. Herbs and spices were also commonly added for flavour and for medicinal purposes, but the defining characteristic of these mead variants is that the majority of the sugar in the fermentation process comes from honey. The various mixtures often have different names in different languages and eras. Some of the most popular melomels, meads made with fruit juices, traditional in the British and Celtic traditions, are cyser (apple juice or cider), morat (mulberries), perry-mead (pear), black mead (blackcurrants) and red mead (redcurrants). A chilli pepper melomel may have been part of ancient Mayan tradition. Straight mead or melomels can also be turned into metheglyn with the addition of herbs or spices. The word itself comes originally from Welsh, suggesting its popularity there, but such meads seem to have been known throughout early Europe. Originally, native grown herbs were used, such as meadowsweet, hops, lavender or chamomile. Once trade between the East and the West was opened up through the Silk Road, spices, such as cinnamon, cloves and nutmeg, were added; combinations were also developed, such as cinnamon cyser.

Mead played an important role in early cultures where it was frequently seen as a gift from the gods. This was possibly because, according to the food historian Bee Wilson, 'though it made them behave like beasts, drinking mead made men feel like gods.'[4] Be that as it may, it was frequently used as a ceremonial offering or libation as well as a refreshment and intoxicant. Pots found in northern China with residue suggesting mead have been dated from 6500 to 7000 BC.[5] Hinduism has the earliest reference to mead, from 3,500 years ago in a text that tells of the Gods of Light using a whip made of mead to bestow life. Early Egyptians and Phoenicians as well as early cultures in Central America also made reference to mead. The Mayans in the Yucatan peninsula region made a type of mead, *balché*, from the honey of the native stingless bee. Believing that bees were a link to the spirit world and that honey was a gift from *Ah Muzen cab*, the bee god, the Mayans used mead in religious rituals. Ancient Greeks and Romans extolled mead's qualities, believing it to be the drink of the gods, who, like mortals, tended to become intoxicated on it and do things that they would not otherwise. According to Plato's *Symposium* (*c.* 360 BC), Love was conceived by Poverty at a feast celebrating the birth of Aphrodite; Poverty slept with the god Resource, who had become tipsy from consuming too much drink.[6] The favoured drinks of these civilizations (and their gods) probably included a variety of forms and combinations of mead, ranging from crude hydromel (simple fermented honey and water) to various combinations of wine and mead, as well as honey used to sweeten and flavour wine.

Mead was common throughout early Eastern Europe and Russia as well as within Celtic, Norse and Germanic tribal cultures. Ancient names for it in some of those cultures come from Indo-European languages rather than the Greek: Germans called it *meth*, Scandinavians *mjod* and Lithuanians *medus*.[7] In Scandinavian mythology, Odin's goat produced mead (*mjod*), and Thor apparently could consume three tons of the beverage. Mead was traditionally featured in numerous other tales and rituals, and some of these have continued into the present. For example, in Finland mead is a celebration drink consumed during the winter season and a special mead, *Simha*, is drunk to celebrate May Day. Although mead seems to have been discovered very early in Europe's history, the skills of fermenting and mixing it with other drinks may not have been introduced until the Roman Empire. Where wild honey was easily available, commoners frequently drank a crude version of it, and housewives were expected to know the skills of making it, along with those of basic beers.

Mead plays a significant role in Russian and Central European history, as it was the primary alcoholic beverage until the fifteenth century. Written references to it date from the eleventh and twelfth centuries, although oral tradition dates it much earlier. Vladimer the Great in AD 996 was said to have included 300 vats of mead in a victory feast – a vat presumably being very large. Such feasts used two types of mead: a lower-quality mead that was brewed in some way using heat, and a matured mead (*med stavlennyi*) that usually included berry juice and would have been left to ferment for ten or more years. Although grapes and wine had also been introduced into these areas and had been gaining in importance, the collapse of the Byzantine Empire along with the Mongol–Tatar invasion between the thirteenth and fifteenth centuries meant a revival of mead making. It became then a drink of the wealthier classes, who preferred the matured meads and left the brewed ones for the commoners. A famous incident from the 1500s in Russia involved Olga of Kiev using mead to intoxicate 5,000 guests at her husband's funeral feast, and then slaying them all. Since honey was becoming less available during the fifteenth century, other substances for making alcoholic beverages were sought. Grains began replacing honey, and other drinks using them gradually took over the role of mead. Later, as potatoes were introduced from the New World to Europe during the so-called 'Columbian Exchange' as a filling and nutritious peasant food, they too became the basis of alcoholic beverages.[8]

Mead figured significantly in the early English and Celtic cultures prior to the Romans introducing it into Europe. The Picts, an Iron Age people from the northern region of Scotland, were making honey ale between 300 and 600 BC.[9] In Irish mythology, the lovers Ossian and Niamh are taken to heaven where rivers flow with mead, and the mythic hero Finn Mac-Cool was refreshed with mead after his demonstrations of strength. Tara, home of the High Kings of Ireland, was called the House of the Mead Circle, and St Brigid miraculously filled a man's vessels with mead so that he could welcome the king. In Wales, the sixth-century poet Taliesin celebrated mead and in the famous *Mabinogion* stories collected from Welsh oral tradition in the twelfth to thirteenth centuries, King Arthur routinely offered mead to visitors as well as to his knights of the Round Table.

The Anglo-Saxon oral epic poem *Beowulf*, the longest epic in Old English, is set in Denmark in a mead hall, where the mead drink apparently enhanced both the enjoyment of feasting and the violence of the brawling. Ruins of mead halls in Denmark from this period have since been found and are now being reconstructed. Archaeologists discovered in the Danish towns of Lejre and Gudme two long oval halls constructed of wood used between AD 660 and 890. These halls would have been significant places for gatherings and would have been centres for the wielding of political power and military might, and mead played an important role in such congregations. It was an important demonstration of hospitality on the part of the host as well as an integral part of any social exchange and celebratory meal. A similar hall has been found in Northumbria, suggesting links between the invading Angles and ninth-century Vikings.

The Canterbury Tales, written by Geoffrey Chaucer at the end of the fourteenth century, similarly refers to the pleasures of mead. In 1669 a manuscript titled *The Closet of the Eminently Learned Sir Kenelm Digbie Opened* listed more than a hundred recipes for mead and its variants – metheglyn, hydromel and honey ale. According to Digbie, metheglyns were certain flavoured meads (which included all sorts of spices, herbs, flowers and fruits), while hydromel – 'honey water' – was just that (honey and water), or extremely weak mead, barely fermented. A recipe that Digbie made especially for the queen included fresh ginger, rosemary and cloves added to 18 quarts (20 litres) of spring water and 1 quart of honey.

Mead apparently played an important role in weddings in the British Isles and Ireland and perhaps helped to create the term 'honeymoon'. It seems to have been common to give newlyweds 'a month's supply of honey wine, or mead, to ensure that married life began as merrily as possible'.[10] An alternative tradition may have been for friends to supply the new husband with mead until he was drunk and then deposit him in bed with his bride. Possibly this was done in the hope that the mead would increase the husband's bravery and make him feel more capable of fulfilling his duties – the expectation was that a son would then be born nine months later.

In much of Europe, mead seems to have spread along with Christianity in the Middle Ages, largely through the establishment of monasteries. The monasteries kept bees, partly for their wax, which was used for the candles necessary for devotions and church rituals. Honey was a convenient and useful by-product of the wax, and was turned into mead, some of which the monasteries would sell to help support their upkeep. Since water was generally considered unsafe to drink, some mead would be kept for the monks to use as a refreshment. The monasteries also made and drank wine for mass. The people then mixed wine with honey or mead, but in some areas, wine replaced mead as the desired and affordable beverage.

Monasteries also kept alive the secrets of good mead making, and some have continued them into the present, despite the waning of mead's popularity. One of the best known is named for the island it inhabits, Lindisfarne, located in Northumbria, northern England, about 112 km (70 miles) south of Edinburgh and separated by a causeway from the mainland. Lindisfarne is one of the most important sites of early Christianity in England. The Irish-born monk St Aiden was brought there from Iona (Scotland) in AD 634 by Oswald, the king of Northumberland. The monastery he established, like most of the monasteries in the British Isles, kept bees, collected honey and made mead. Lindisfarne is famous, though, for maintaining its traditions into the present, and today, St Aidan's Winery produces mead said to be made from the original recipe. Its mead is technically more of a melomel or even a metheglyn, since it is concocted from grape juice, honey, local spring water and herbs.

Mead and Honey Drinks Today

European mead is popular today as a heritage drink. A number of festivals celebrate mead, and it is frequently found at Renaissance and medieval re-enactments and fairs.[11] Bunratty Castle in County Clare in the Republic of Ireland, for example, offers both mead and honey liqueurs in its shop and on its menu for its re-enactment feasts held in the castle. Ideally, in such situations, mead is served in earthenware goblets to evoke an earlier, much romanticized time. Similarly, warmed mulled meads and spiced honey wines are now associated with winter festivities.

Mead seems to be enjoying a comeback due to current trends in local food production, natural foods, home brewing and beekeeping. In 2014 there were more than 150 meaderies in the United States, and an American Meadmakers Association was formally created in 2012. It is a versatile drink, although not to everyone's taste, and many find it either too flat or too sweet.[12] It also can be expensive to make, since honey itself can now be quite pricey to buy. With a ratio of 1 part honey to 4 parts water, a fairly large amount of honey is needed to make any real quantity of mead. Be that as it may, a collection of recipes taken from the *Mead Lover's Digest* in 1994 lists more than twenty varieties made with fruit, spices, grapes, apples and lemons along with a variety of flavourings.[13] Mead will most likely gain in popularity, as will other drinks containing honey, as honey itself regains its original position as the world's first and most natural sweetener.

5
Honey for Health and Healing

My Son, eat thou honey, for it is good.
King Solomon

The fruit of bees is desired by all, and is equally sweet
to kings and beggars and it is not only pleasing but profitable
and healthful; it sweetens their mouths, cures their wounds,
and conveys remedies to inward ulcers.
St Ambrose

Honey not only helps disguise the bitter flavour of medicine and soothes the throat, but is frequently used as a medicine by itself. Historically, it was used throughout the world for numerous health-related reasons – as a medicinal substance, protection against disease and misfortune, an energizer, a general tonic and source of strength as well as a beauty enhancer for skin and hair. Many of these uses have carried into the present day as alternative health practices, old wives' tales or folk remedies. While some of these customary uses were associated with legends of the divine nature of honey, many were based on experience and observation. Today, honey is associated with natural and organic foods and alternative health beliefs; other bee products, such as bee pollen, propolis

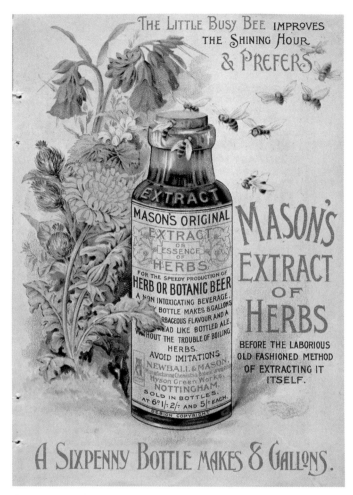

Advertisement for herbal extract with bees swarming around the bottle, indicating its sweetness and healthful qualities, 19th century.

and royal jelly, are frequently promoted along with it. A new branch of alternative medicine in the West, apitherapy, has recently developed around honey and bee products, and is drawing upon the knowledge of the many non-Western medical systems that have long used honey.

Scientific studies have shown that honey does have some healing and medicinal powers, although there is still much debate within the medical community surrounding the validity of such studies. Many of them have been done outside the established medical community, and therefore are not fully recognized. An influential medical website states, 'But outside of the laboratory, claims for honey's healthfulness are unproven – except in the area of wound care and, to a lesser extent, cough suppression.'[1] This lack of attention to honey's healing powers and health potential probably reflects long-standing biases in Western thought and medicine that make the establishment suspicious of the natural world in general, and of seemingly non-scientific approaches to taking care of the body. The food writer Bee Wilson, however, points out that the hesitancy to accept honey's medical efficacy might be due partly to the enthusiasm with which some people have embraced it: 'Unfortunately, many of the other claims made on behalf of hive products in the past were nothing but crazed quackery.'[2] Despite this, traditional practices using honey for health and healing have continued among various groups throughout the world, and those practices have recently been drawing attention.

A cautionary note: honey can pose some potential dangers. It can cause botulism in infants, and nectars from toxic plants that do not usually harm bees can be turned into honey poisonous to humans. Also, contemporary commercial honey is sometimes mixed with other substances, diluting its effectiveness in alleviating health problems.

Furthermore, honey that has been filtered and processed, as much commercial honey has been, is said by some to lose much of its medicinal effectiveness. Raw honey is recommended, then, for health uses, but is not as readily available and tends to be expensive.

Historical Uses of Honey for Medicine and Health

While the use of honey for health reasons has most likely occurred since humans first began to consume it, the earliest evidence is from the Egyptians, around 5,000 years ago, who used it to treat wounds. (They also used honey to embalm the dead, but that was obviously for a non-health-related function.) The ancient Egyptians considered it a healthy food, especially for babies, and honey seemed to be thought of in general as a protector against illness or evil (which frequently displayed itself as disease). Such beliefs were common in most other cultures familiar with honey.

Ayurvedic medicine, originating in ancient India 4,000 years ago, prescribed honey as a cure for, among other things, intestinal and urinary tract disorders, nausea, asthma and impotence; it was also thought to improve eyesight and help control weight. Raw honey was also used as a laxative. The sacred hymns, the Vedas, speak of honey as a source of a long life and good health. According to Stephen Buchmann, a ceremony for newborn males in India included anointing them with honey and reciting: 'I give thee this honey food so that the gods may protect thee, and that thou mayst live a hundred autumns in this world.'[3] Such rituals are found throughout history, and examples have been described from a wide range of cultures, including those of the West Indies, Samoa,

Advertisement for Chinese honey medicine, 1503–5.

本草品彙精要卷之二十九

蟲魚部上品

石蜜 無毒

蜀州蜜

Burma, Pakistan, Scotland, Finland, Greece, the Caucasus, India, African nations and Germany.[4]

The Greeks and Romans similarly referred to honey's power to heal wounds and illnesses and believed that consuming honey contributed to a person's longevity. The fourth-century BC philosophers Aristotle and Aristoxenus both commended honey. It was understood to be a source of energy and was consumed by athletes in the ancient Olympic Games in order to enhance performance. Pliny the Elder, around the first century AD, suggested mixing honey with 'powdered bees' to cure dropsy, constipation, urinary tract and bladder infections, and kidney stones. He also advised that consuming raw honey was an effective laxative, but boiling it would cure diarrhoea, and that honey from toxic plants could cure epilepsy.

King Solomon in the Old Testament seemed to encourage people to eat honey for their health, claiming 'My Son, eat thou honey, for it is good' (Proverbs 24:13) – although its goodness can also refer to its taste and sweetness. The many references to the Promised Land as one of milk and honey, though, suggests that honey represented abundance, fertility and well-being.

Similarly, the Qu'ran states that 'There comes from within [the bee] a beverage of many colours, in which there is healing for men' (16:69), and the Prophet Mohammad claimed that 'Honey is a remedy for every illness of the body and the Quran is a remedy for all illnesses of the mind. Therefore I recommend to you both remedies, the Quran and honey.'[5]

Early European cultures also treated honey as a tonic, medicine and protector against disease. They used it as an ointment on wounds and applied it to the skin, partly to help hold the skin together or in place, but also to help healing. Burns were frequently treated topically with honey, and honey was consumed as a tonic for good health. Various concoctions were recorded, such as honey and pigeon dung mixed together to treat kidney stones; Hippocrates' recipe from the fifth century BC of 'powdered viper' sweetened with honey, which was re-used centuries later for protection against the Plague that decimated populations in the mid-1300s; and an English ointment from the mid-1440s that called for duck grease, turpentine, soot, molasses, egg yolks and scorpion oil mixed with honey.[6]

Honey was also used in Europe to 'sweeten' the task of collecting 'night soil' – human faeces – that had to be carried away from homes to be deposited outside. The poor souls conducting the task would wrap cloths soaked in honey around their mouths and nostrils, hence the term 'honey bucket' for the pots used for the waste.

Contemporary Remedies

Although honey is not officially used as a medicine in mainstream Western cultures, it is still a frequent home remedy, especially stirred into hot drinks for sore throats, and the flavour, if not the actual substance, is used in throat lozenges. Honey's smooth texture also helps substances go down the throat, making it easier to swallow. Various preparations for

'Preparation of Medicine from Honey', 1224, from an Arabic translation of the *Materia Medica* of Dioscorides (AD 50–70), Baghdad School, Iraq.

skin- and haircare products, lip balms and moisturizers use honey, and some people consume it specifically for energy. Recommendations from a number of sources claim that it cures or helps manage a multitude of diseases or conditions, including impotence, ulcers, bacterial gastroenteritis, heart disease, bronchial asthma, urinary tract disorders, diarrhoea, eye problems, some cancers, diabetes, coughs, high cholesterol, allergies, menopause, colds, ear infections, pneumonia, tuberculosis, meningitis, respiratory infections, diphtheria and so on. It is claimed to fight infections in general, to boost the immune system, provide energy, speed up the growth of new tissue and help with weight gain as well as weight loss. Some people swear by a daily tablespoon of raw honey for good health and long life. Enthusiasts also point out that it

Honey-based cosmetics, soaps and creams are popularly marketed in the u.s. as being naturally healthy and eco-friendly.

Czech advertisement for honey-based cough medicine.

does all of these without side effects and at a fraction of the cost of most pharmaceuticals. Other bee products – propolis, royal jelly, bee pollen and even beeswax – are similarly promoted and sometimes mixed with honey. Royal jelly, in particular, is touted as having health benefits ranging from preventing some types of cancers, lowering blood pressure and cholesterol, and healing digestive disorders to increasing fertility, relieving symptoms of the menopause and preventing premature ageing. Few scientific studies have been conducted to corroborate these claims.

Healthful and Healing Properties of Honey

So do any of these claims of honey's powers have credibility? Numerous studies have examined honey to identify and analyse its medicinal and health benefits. The properties, however, depend largely on the particular type and quality of flowers from which the bees collected the nectar that is then turned into honey. Most studies agree that healthy and organic flowers produce nectar with more nutrients, and the darker the colour of the honey, the more antioxidants and less water it contains, so the healthier it is. Unfortunately the darker varieties of honey also tend to be the most expensive and are not easily found – some of these varieties are also considered too robust and less tasty.

Several types of honey are especially known for their medicinal and health uses. Buckwheat honey, for example, has more antioxidants than the more common sage and clover honeys.[7] Buckwheat honeys from Eastern Europe are advertised for their health-giving properties and are frequently stocked in health food shops. A type of honey from New Zealand, manuka honey made from the nectar of *Leptospermum scoparium*, has been particularly touted for its health benefits, with studies claiming that it kills bacteria and helps to prevent as well as heal infections. In 2007 the U.S. Food and Drug Administration approved a topical ointment made from manuka honey, Medihoney, for use on wounds. A website is quick to point out, though, that Medihoney can be painful when applied, so should not be used on burns.[8]

Another variety thought to have especially high medicinal properties is also one of the most expensive honeys in the world. Sidr honey comes from the sidr trees found in the Hadramaut Mountains of Yemen and Saudi Arabia. The trees themselves are considered holy in Islam and are believed to be thousands of years old. Legends claim that its fruit (jujube) was the first food eaten by Adam. Honey from bees that collect nectar from the sidr tree is believed to be unusually healthy and good for curing numerous ailments. There are even claims that, mixed with other substances, such as carrot seeds or ginseng, it is an aphrodisiac. Another special honey from New Zealand is said to be higher than others in minerals. Beech honeydew honey originates from the secretions of aphids living in beech trees, rather than from the nectar of flowers. The methods used for processing honey also affect its qualities, with raw honey containing more of the phytochemicals that fight against bacteria, viruses and fungi. Raw honey also usually contains small amounts of propolis and bee pollen, both thought by some to have health-giving properties. Honey also has varying effects if it is taken internally or applied topically, and different needs call for different treatments.

Buckwheat honey purchased from a Ukrainian grocery store in the Cleveland area, Ohio.

'Clonmel, Cluain-Meala, the meadow of the honey', cigarette card, early 20th century.

Honey has been shown – both through folk knowledge and scientific studies – to have antibacterial, antiseptic and antibiotic properties, but the actual processes may differ according to the type of honey. Acording to some studies, most honeys contain an enzyme, a protein called bee defensing-1, that produces hydrogen peroxide, which kills any bacteria.[9] Even those varieties not containing that enzyme can protect against bacteria. One study suggests that the low pH level and high sugar content may be responsible.[10] Others claim that honey contains an agent called inhibine that kills bacteria when applied topically. Honey also acts as an antioxidant by removing or damaging oxidizing agents that cause deterioration of organic materials. According to one study, the slightly acidic pH level of honey (between 3.2 and 4.5) helps prevent the growth of bacteria, while its antioxidant constituents cleans up free radicals.[11] Honey's hygroscopic character also aids in healing. Hygroscopic refers to the ability to attract and absorb water molecules from the surrounding environment, usually the air. Honey draws moisture from a wound, keeping it from providing a place conducive to the growth of bacteria. It also dehydrates the bacteria themselves, killing them or rendering them ineffective.[12]

Honey further assists in healing because of its viscosity. Its thick, sticky, semi-fluid consistency allows it to spread easily over wounds, slipping into crevasses in the skin, so that the pushing and prodding of ointments into the body is unnecessary. It then creates a topical barrier that prevents airborne bacteria entering into a wound. It also serves as an effective adhesive for bandages, causing them to stick and stay in place, but allowing them to be removed and changed without further damaging the skin or hindering new cell growth. The bandages peel off the honey rather than the skin. Consuming honey may reduce pain, although there is no proven identification of the properties that work in such a process. Studies on the use of honey after tonsillectomy operations among children demonstrated that it helped to relieve the pain experienced. It was administered along with other analgesics rather than replacing them completely, but made a significant difference.[13]

A popular belief about honey is that it is an allergen suppressant. Although the medical establishment debates this, the theory remains that since honey is made from the nectar of flowering plants, it contains minuscule amounts of the properties of those nectars. Ingesting that honey, then, gives immunity to individuals suffering from allergies to thos same plants, or at least alleviates their reactions. Local honeys are considered best for this purpose and, ideally, honeys can be selected for allergies to specific plants. Some people suggest consuming honey prior to the times of the year when allergens tend to be in the air as a preventative measure against reactions. The bee pollen – that is, the male cells of nectars – is also considered 'a nutritive tonic' that can 'desensitize seasonal allergies'.[14]

Apart from its medicinal uses, honey has long been considered a tonic that can restore health and energy and maintain general well-being. It is an excellent source of energy, being made up principally of sugars. It has both glucose and fructose, with more of the latter, along with traces of 22 to 25 other sugars (oligosaccharides). Honey is denser and heavier

The Edwin Smith papyrus, the world's oldest surviving surgical document, written in hieratic script in ancient Egypt around 1600 BC. Among the treatments described are closing wounds with sutures, preventing and curing infection with honey and mouldy bread and stopping bleeding with raw meat.

MINERAL	LIGHT HONEY (p.p.m.)	DARK HONEY (p.p.m.)
Potassium	205	1,676
Chlorine	52	113
Sulphur	58	100
Calcium	49	51
Sodium	18	76
Phosphorus	35	47
Magnesium	19	35
Silica	22	36
Iron	2.4	9.4
Manganese	0.30	4.09
Copper	0.29	0.56

than sugar, and although a tablespoon of honey contains 68 calories whereas a tablespoon of sugar has 49, the former is still considered healthier by some people because of the types of sugar making up honey. Different types of honey contain different ratios of these sugars as well as varying traces of minerals.[15]

The Dangers of Honey: Botulism and Allergies

Honey for centuries was considered a healthy food for babies and children. It has only very recently acquired an association with danger, and this is largely due to a discovery made in 1976.

It turns out that occasionally honey contains *Clostridium botulism* spores, which can cause botulism in infants. While these pose no danger for adults and older children whose digestive tracts have matured, they can be a risk for younger children who have not yet acquired that immunity. Reactions to botulism can run from mild to severe, and in a small number of cases may result in death. For that reason, the American medical establishment advises against giving honey to babies less than one year of age. The u.s. Department of Health and Human Services states, clearly: 'Do not let babies eat honey.'[16] The National Honey Board follows this guideline and includes a warning on every jar of honey to not feed it to infants under the age of one, stating: 'The concern for babies stems from the fact that infants lack the fully developed gastrointestinal tract of older humans.'

Not everyone agrees with that conclusion, especially in light of the thousands of years in which honey was used as an apparently healthy food source for babies. Conclusions about honey causing botulism may have been based on a few cases in which other contaminants actually caused the botulism; the number of cases, it seems, has been negligible, with the bulk of them in California. Sugar has since replaced honey as a sweetener for children, perhaps reflecting the ongoing power of the sugar industry to offer its product at a lower price than honey. The shift in attitudes towards honey over time can be seen in a postcard from 1884 showing a baby cherub riding a carriage pulled by bees with the words 'Sweetness & Health' beneath.[17] Other advertising and food labels prior to the 1970s similarly touted the benefits of honey to babies.

A less controversial caution over consuming honey is specifically for people who are known to have an allergy to bee stings. The stings carry poison (known as apitoxin or apis virus) that can cause anaphylactic shock, with reactions ranging from mild to severe respiratory distress and even death. Those individuals who know they are allergic to bee venom frequently carry a medication, epinephrine, to counter the effects and, while apitoxin is not usually found in honey, people with an extreme allergy to it may take precautions with honey and other bee products. Individuals with allergies to conifer and poplar trees might also need to be cautious when consuming honey gathered from areas where those trees are known to grow.[18] Honey contains small amounts of oxalates, which may exacerbate kidney stones, although raw honey with vinegar or lemon juice is a traditional treatment for dissolving these stones.

Toxic and Hallucinogenic Honey

Honey made from the nectars of flowers that are toxic to humans can be poisonous; known varieties include oleanders, azalea, the Carolina jasmine, southern leatherwood, loco-weed, jimson weed, tansy ragwort, rhododendron, mountain laurel and boxwood. Usually these plants are not harmful to bees, but some are reported to be, such as a variety of horse chestnut in California.[19] Symptoms to humans who have come into contact with poisonous honey can include vomiting, diarrhoea, dizziness, lack of control over limbs (similar to drunkenness, so the sufferers stagger when moving) and hallucination. It can even be fatal.

The ancients were familiar with toxic honey. The Greeks called it maddening honey and were therefore cautious of eating wild honey.[20] Aristotle even wrote of boxwood honey in Asia Minor that would make people go mad (but would cure epilepsy) and Ovid warned of hemlock honey. Pliny the Elder described deadly honey and pointed to Asia Minor, Persia and North Africa as locations for such honey. Toxic honey was perhaps the explanation for the behaviour of John the Baptist, who survived his time in the wilderness by eating locusts and wild honey, but was described in the Old Testament as somewhat odd, wearing unusual garments made from camel's hair and leather, publicly condemning those in power and preaching of the coming of Jesus.[21] As mentioned in Chapter One, such honey was given to invading soldiers in the Mediterranean in 401 BC and 67 BC. In modern times, the city of Philadelphia suffered an outbreak in 1790 of sickness and death caused by honey made from the poisonous nectar of mountain laurel.[22]

Some honey has been intentionally used as a hallucinogen. The ancient Mayans possibly gave it to sacrificial victims, who would subsequently be rendered unaware of their grisly fates. Today, the Gurung people living in the Himalayan mountain region, primarily in Nepal, gather wild honey from an unusually large and aggressive variety of bee that is known to cause hallucinations. Climbing rock cliffs to reach nests and facing dangerous swarms of these bees, the 'honey hunters' then use the honey for medicinal and ritualistic purposes. Videos and photographs of the Gurung honey traditions abound on the Internet and have sensationalized them, drawing numerous visitors to the area who seek the effects of 'Red Honey', as it is called.

The easiest way to avoid toxic honey is to refrain from eating honey gathered from the nests of wild bees, since the source of that honey is unknown. Today though, toxic honey tends to not be considered a health or safety issue among beekeepers. Most know the flowering plants that their bees feed upon, and if they live in the vicinity of poisonous plants they can discard the honey made from those nectars. They can also time the harvesting of honey to lessen any possibilities of toxic nectars contaminating their supply.

Conclusion

Honey's health benefits seem to far outweigh any dangers, as long as the consumer exercises some reasonable caution. The test of time seems to support some claims to honey's curative powers, and the medical establishment seems to be opening up more to its possibilities and is conducting scientific studies of the efficacy of various claims. I leave it up to readers to draw their own conclusions, but end with a quotation from a contemporary promotion for honey:

> Caution: Those that make Honey a regular part of their diet often experience a feeling of extreme well-being and a feeling that all is right with the world. Such symptoms are normal and should not be confused with psychic disorders.[23]

6

Honey as Art and Symbol in Folk and Popular Culture

Honey has played a significant role not only in the foodways of numerous cultures throughout history but in their religious beliefs, rituals and social life. Some of this role has carried over to the present so that honey appears as a symbol and motif in folk and popular art forms. It has also been incorporated into our vocabulary in various ways as a term of endearment, an adjective and in metaphors.[1] The meanings attached to honey, while usually suggesting affection and goodness, can also be contradictory: lust as well as love; honesty or deceitfulness; the sweetness but also the stickiness or complexity of life. (The symbolism of bees is even more complex, but that is the subject of another book.)

The Etymology of 'Honey'

The terms used to name honey in different languages reflect its long history – and significance – in human cultures throughout the world. Many share common roots. Linguists have determined that the word for honey in Proto-Indo-European, which is believed to be the original language source for most European and Sanskrit languages, was *melit*. This evolved into the Greek *melis*, Latin *mel* and Sanskrit *madhu*. The Chinese word for honey, *mi*, may have the same origin. The Greek and Latin words turned into contemporary French *miel*, Italian *miele*, Portuguese *mel*, Spanish *miel*, Welsh *mèl* and Irish *mil*. The Latin *mel* is a root for numerous words in English: Melpomene, the Greek muse of tragedy, melodrama, melody, melon, mellifluous, mellow (meaning rich in flavour) and the name Melissa (Greek for 'honeybee').

Meanwhile the Sanskrit word *madhu* seems to have influenced not only South Asian and Southeast Asian languages, but even Slavic and Central European ones. Honey in Hindi is *madhu*, and in Malay and Indonesian, *madu*. In Polish, it is *miòd*; Latvian, *medus*; Lituanian, *medus*; Hungarian, *méz*; and Czech, *med*. The English word *mead*, a fermented honey drink, seems to have developed from those sources.

A whole different family of words for 'honey' comes from the proto-German *humagam*, which seems to have derived from the Indo-European *k(e)neko*, meaning yellow or golden. This turned into German *honig*, Icelandic *hunang*, Norwegian *honning* and Dutch *honing*. The contemporary English word 'honey' evolved from the Old English *hunig*, which became *honi*.

As an aside, Basque, spoken in northeastern Spain and unrelated to any surrounding languages, uses the word *eztia*, affirming the autonomous status of the language and culture. Similarly, the Korean word for honey, *kool*, is unique, demonstrating Korean as a 'language isolate' with no known relative. Although Korean has adopted many Chinese words, its use of its own term for honey implies that honey as a food developed there indigenously. Similarly, honey in Japanese, *hachimitsu*, seems unrelated to either Chinese or Korean.

The Symbolism of Honey

Honey is often thought of today as symbolic of sweetness and affection, but those are not its only meanings, particularly historically. The ancient Greeks associated honey with lust (maybe partly due to the effects of mead), but bees with virginity – as did many people throughout the Middle Ages. The lustful connotation of honey still appears in the present day, although it seems to be somewhat watered down to a name for women.

Meanwhile, the usage of the word honey in the Old Testament reveals several meanings common among the ancient Hebrews.[2] It could stand for acquiring wisdom and a good reputation: 'Behold, a virgin shall conceive and bear a son, and shall call his name Immanuel. Butter and honey shall he eat, that he may know to refuse the evil and choose the good.' (Isaiah 7:15) As for the Greeks, it could also represent temptation and be a tool for deceit, seen in the expressions 'honey under the tongue' and 'venom under the tongue'. As the opposite of temptation, honey was used as a symbol of restraint and moderation against over-indulgence, a meaning that does not seem to have carried over into the present. The Old Testament also referred to the Promised Land as a 'land of milk and honey', a place of abundance and peace. Offered to Moses as a reward after wandering the desert for forty years, this description also harkens back to Eden, where humankind could be sustained by nature without having to labour for its fruits.

Much of the symbolism attached to honey in the past emerges in many ways today. In the sixteenth century William Shakespeare alluded to its mundane origins in his play *King Henry V*: 'Thus may we gather honey from the weed, and make a moral of the devil himself' (Act IV, scene 1). Although we usually associate honey with flowers, some of those flowers, such as clover, are thought of as weeds. Yet the nectars from those weeds result in something quite healthful and tasty. Also, the sweetness of honey is frequently compared to speaking sweetly or having a sweet disposition. As early as 1732 a book published in London by Thomas Fuller, *Gnomologia: Adagies and Proverbs; Wise Sentences and Witty Sayings, Ancient and Modern, Foreign and British*, included the proverb, 'more flies are taken with a drop of honey than a tun of vinegar.' Benjamin Franklin gave a variation of this in his *Poor Richard's Almanack*, published in 1759: 'Tart words make no friends: a spoonful of honey will catch more flies than a gallon of vinegar.' Probably much older is a similar Arabic proverb: 'When you shoot an arrow of truth, dip its point in honey.' These sayings use honey as a metaphor for good manners, a sweet nature and considerate social interactions.

Such sweetness, however, can also be deceptive. Franklin's admonition in his *Almanack* that 'If you have no honey in your pot, have some in your mouth' suggests that sweetness is needed to get what one needs and therefore might be insincere. 'Honey-tongued', today, refers to someone who speaks dishonestly but pleasantly.

'Honeypot' is used to denote a computer program designed to trap other users or computers that are trying to break into another information system, and an earlier usage – popularized in acts of espionage – referred to a seductive person who had been planted in enemy territory. 'Honey buckets' are indoor containers used as a toilet without plumbing. They can be as simple as a mere bucket or may have more elaborate designs, but the main point is that they have to then be carried out of the house to be emptied. Their use in Korea is particularly notorious, because during and after the Korean War the idea of the honey bucket was used in American mass

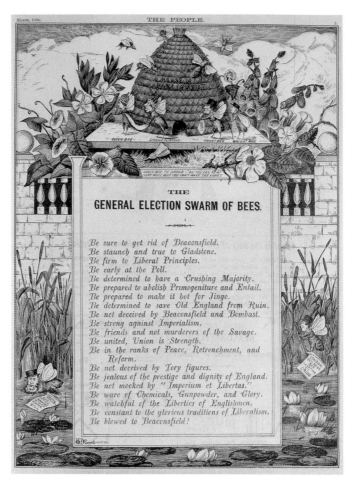

Political cartoon showing Queen Victoria, Benjamin Disraeli and other political figures depicted as bees around a beehive representing the Houses of Parliament. Engraving by W. D. Ewan, 1880.

'The wasps and the honey-pot', cigarette card, early 20th century.

media and entertainment to propagate an image of Korean culture as backwards.

Imitation rather than deception appears in the use of 'honey' as an adjective for plants that taste as sweet as honey: honeysuckle vines, honey locust trees, honeydew melon. Similarly, honeydew is a sweet residue found on plants in early morning – similar to the dew left by the night's moisture. It is actually the excrement of aphids, but is as sweet as honey and consumed as such. It is possible that what the Israelites thought was sent by God as manna was actually honeydew. Honeydew can be turned into honey when it is picked up by bees as nectar. In Germany's Black Forest region it is called forest or fir honey, and in France it is 'flea honey' or *miel de puce*. Similarly, bees in New Zealand make honeydew honey from the secretions of insects that live in tree bark. The flavour is said to be 'pungent'.[3]

Honey as Lust, Love and Romance

Honey's sweetness has been likened to an aphrodisiac, but whether that is deception or not is a matter of opinion. The Book of Genesis, chapter 41, mentions an Egyptian woman, Asenath, who seduces Joseph by giving him 'the whitest of honey combs'. (In her defence, he was 'aroused' when he heard that no other man had touched her.[4]) A ninth-century Irish legend similarly alludes to honey's seductive powers in an offer by the hero to a woman: 'Your thirst shall be slaked with the finest mead, and your dish be filled with limpid honey.'[5]

The ancient Greek symbolism of honey for lust is today more likely to be seen in cultures of the West in the names and descriptions of women who might represent objects of lust. As a stage name (or alias) for women in nightclubs, films or other popular mediums, it carries associations of seduction and sensual pleasure. The word is also used in creating allure, as in an eye shadow shade named 'honey lust', and a line of jewellery titled 'Honey Lust Jewelry'.

The association of honey with procreation and fertility – which can be thought of as a result of love – was a familiar motif in ancient cultures. Rivers in the Promised Land flowed with milk and honey, and Astarte, the Greek goddess (called Ishtar in Mesopotamia) of fertility, maternity, love and war, gave honey as a gift to her people. Cupid or Eros, the classical gods of love, had arrows that were sometimes dipped in honey, representing both the sweetness and pain (or sting) of love. This last idea has been the subject of paintings showing Cupid stealing honey, such as a work of *c.* 1525 by Lucas Cranach, showing a baby Cupid holding honeycomb with bees crawling on him, next to a beautiful and naked young woman, Venus, his mother.

Lucas Cranach, *Cupid Complaining to Venus*, c. 1525. Cupid is being stung by bees while stealing their honeycomb and complaining to Venus.

Jan Matthias Cok (1735–1771), 'L'Amour piqué': Cupid stung by a bee while stealing honey, or while picking a rose.

Starting in ancient Greece, honey cakes were material expressions of beliefs about honey and love. They were offered to the gods for fertility, and in medieval Europe they were given by girls to men as keepsakes in the form of heart-shaped spice cakes. A small mirror and sayings might have been pressed into it, and the cake was expected to be preserved and not eaten. Similar honey cakes were also funeral souvenirs, perhaps a purer expression of affection. The tradition has continued into the present in Austria and Germany, where gingerbread (actually, honey cakes) are still made and eaten at Christmas.

One of the most romantic times of a person's life is named after honey: the honeymoon. There are several theories for the name of this period of seclusion and privacy after a wedding. In Celtic tradition, the month of May was when the honey was harvested to be made into mead, so the full moon was referred to as the honeymoon. Tradition also held that weddings occurred on the first of May, so the moon name was attached to the days after the wedding – and probably linked to the tradition of mead drinking as well. Mead seems to have been given as a gift to newlyweds, perhaps to give courage to the new groom, or to smooth the transition for both parties. Another theory is that Norse gods harvested

REFLECTIONS ON MATRIMONY.
THE HONEY MOON,
AND AFTERWARDS.

Theodore Lane, 'Reflections on Matrimony: The Honey Moon and Afterwards', 19th-century engraving.

honey and made it into wine, then set aside a time to use that wine for romantic pursuits.[6]

Honey's double meanings, though, also appear in references to love. Shakespeare, no less, observed in *Romeo and Juliet* that its sweetness could cover up other qualities, perhaps in the way that being in love tends to make us blind to unattractive characteristics of the loved one: 'The sweetest honey is loathsome in its own deliciousness and in the taste confounds the appetite, therefore love moderately' (Act II, scene VI). Honey's sweetness, as here described by Friar Laurence, alludes to both love and deceit.

A Term of Endearment and Affection

'Honey' has been used as a term of endearment in Europe since the mid-fourteenth century and perhaps earlier.[7] Although more often thought of as referring to females, today it is commonly used regardless of gender, age or even relationship. Spouses and romantic partners frequently refer to each other as 'honey', as do parents to their children. In popular culture, it tends to be a male referring to a female partner or spouse, as in the popularized phrase 'Honey, I'm home', or in the title of the American family film *Honey, I Shrunk the Kids* (1989). It also appears in traditional and popular music, for example the old-time Appalachian tune 'Ain't Got no Honeybabe Now', sung by the twentieth-century guitar player and singer Doc Watson. Blues musicians frequently associated honey with kisses (and suggested other activities as well). In keeping with that tradition, the blues great Muddy Waters sang lyrics featuring honey that were popularized by the Rolling Stones in their song 'I Want to Be Loved'. A twist on the term is seen in the phrase 'honey do list' for a list of chores for a husband to do.

In a twist on the gender dynamic of using 'honey' to express affection, in the American South it is common for women, most famously waitresses in restaurants, to refer to all customers as 'honey'. In Baltimore, Maryland, an entire festival has grown up around the shortened form of 'honey' ('hon') as a term of endearment for customers: the HonFest, which began in 1994 and includes a specific hairstyle (fittingly the beehive) and outfit.

Honey is also used to describe a woman's personality in a positive way, as in Van Morrison's song 'Tupelo Honey'. Tupelo honey has a distinctive taste and is a more expensive variety than many, so the song's reference to it can be understood as a compliment. Similarly, the phrase 'she's a honey' refers to a woman who behaves in a sweet and kind way. The famous British author Roald Dahl named a character after the food in his children's novel *Matilda* (1988). Miss Jennifer Honey was a kind teacher; an unusual quality for an adult in Dahl's writing. The American Association of School Librarians gives an award named after her, the Miss Honey Social Justice Award, to librarians who seek to collaborate with and support teachers.

Honey in Oral and Written Literature and the Media

Honey often appears in titles of romance novels in English-language literature, seeming to refer to sweetness and its associations with affection and love. Also, since it was a common food historically, honey is found in European folk myths and legends as a feature of everyday life. 'Treyosha', a Russian tale by Alexei Tolstoy, includes an example in which a mother calls her son with the refrain: 'Come and eat your lunch, Teryosha sonny, / There's milk, and curds, and bread and honey!' In the story, a witch imitates the mother's voice and tricks the boy into coming to her instead.[8]

Honey plays a role in a number of children's books – probably the most famous is Winnie-the-Pooh, by A. A. Milne. In the four volumes originally published between 1924 and 1928, and in the subsequent Disney animations, Pooh is notorious for his love of honey, as seen in one conversation with his human friend, Christopher Robin:

> 'What do you like doing best in the world, Pooh?'
>
> 'Well,' said Pooh, 'what I like best-' and then he had to stop and think. Because although Eating Honey was a very good thing to do, there was a moment just before you began to eat it which was better than when you were, but he didn't know what it was called.

Pooh is also a bit of a philosopher, although a rather fatalistic one. Honey comes into that in *The House at Pooh*

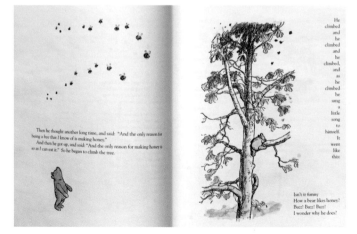

Then he thought another long time, and said: "And the only reason for being a bee that I know of is making honey."
And then he got up, and said: "And the only reason for making honey is so as I can eat it." So he began to climb the tree.

He climbed and he climbed and he climbed, and as he climbed he sang a little song to himself. It went like this:

Isn't it funny
How a bear likes honey?
Buzz! Buzz! Buzz!
I wonder why he does?

The gorgeous E. H. Shepard illustrated version of *Winnie the Pooh* by A. A. Milne.

F. Barlow delin.   Ja.ˢ Kirk fecit.

A Bee's keen Sting a Bear did so enrage,   The Numbers join, and on their Foe do fall,
That, with the Hives, a War he does engage: Who grieves his private Feud prov'd national.

MORAL.

So petty Tumults, by the Rout pursu'd,
Have often mighty Commonwealths subdu'd.

Bears have long been associated with honey. In this Russian cartoon, a
bear is stung by bees when he tries to steal their honey.

Corner (1928): 'The only reason for being a bee that I know of
is making honey . . . and the only reason for making honey is
so I can eat it.'

Walt Disney popularized Milne's work, introducing Pooh
into the mass media in 1966 as a cartoon character and depict-
ing him carrying a pot of honey. This image of Pooh and his
honey jar is frequently found on products for children –
clothing, home furnishings, dishware, toys and more. Another
cartoon bear who liked honey was Yogi Bear, created by
William Hanna and Joseph Barbera in 1958. Famous in television cartoons and comic books, Yogi is usually portrayed
eating honey straight from the jar or from nests in the wild.
Yogi's sidekick, a little bear named Boo Boo, aids him in

Wenceslaus Hollar (1607–1677), *The Bear and the Honey*, etching.

acquiring honey, a task that frequently gets them both into trouble. The sidekick's name was then used in an American television reality show that started in 2012 about a little girl competing in beauty pageants, *Here Comes Honey Boo Boo*. The title also plays on 'honey' as a term of endearment.

'Honey' appears in numerous other artistic contexts – literature, music, the visual arts and theatre. It frequently is

MUSCOVITE CAUTION.

RUSSIA.— I would like to have the honey, but I 'm afraid of the bees!

Bears' love of honey appears in this political cartoon of a 'Muscovite Bear' yearning after a British beehive, 1900.

J. E. Ridinger, honey-trap for a bear in the forest, early 18th century, etching.

simply part of the scenery, so to speak, with other foods, but connotations of sweetness as well as other meanings – seduction, deceit – are often attached to it. The influential contemporary American all-female gospel group Sweet Honey in the Rock based their name on Psalm 81:16 in the Bible: 'Sweet Honey speaks of a land that is so rich, when you break the rocks open honey flows. And we thought it was something like us African-American women . . . strong like a rock but inside [there's] honey – sweet.'⁹

Material Culture Surrounding Honey

Another aspect of honey that includes an artistic turn is found in an unexpected place – the containers for it. These are often ceramic pots of a similar size to a sugar bowl, with a removable lid, but with an opening for a utensil designed especially for serving honey. These utensils, frequently shaped like a beehive and made of wood or metal, allow the honey to be removed from the jar without dripping (that is, in theory). These ceramics are made in England, Japan and the United States, often in shapes that evoke old-fashioned and folk lifestyles or that represent the connection of honey to bees, such as beehive-shaped bowls, or ceramics with bees painted on or bee-shaped embellishments attached. Bears

Decorated honey jar, 1871–93; honey pot and stand, 1798–9.

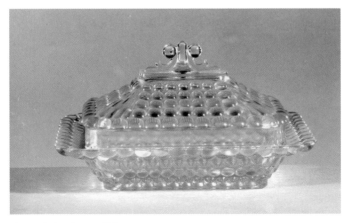

Covered glass honey dish, 1870–90.

The Beehive House, Salt Lake City, Utah.

are another popular motif and form for these. Poland, in particular, has a long tradition of ornately painted jars.

Other types of honey jars are made of glass, including one with a small bowl underneath to hold hot water to keep the honey free-flowing. The jars themselves are frequently of interesting and distinctive shapes and designs. Crystal jars with crystal, metal or even silver tops, for example, were the standard for good taste in dishware in Russia and other areas of Eastern Europe dating back at least to the mid-1800s. Wooden and metal containers were also used, and these came in a variety of designs. An antique silver honeypot from Russia, for example, was made to look like birch bark.[10]

The artistic design of honeypots was and is perhaps partly for marketing purposes, but it also suggests the importance of honey in the food traditions of those cultures during the eighteenth and nineteenth centuries. The designs made the jars suitable for display on a dinner table or with other fine dishware. Today, honeypots are likely to be displayed along with a tea set or at breakfast time, the meal at which honey is most often eaten. Also, small jars of honey are popular souvenirs and gifts, including being given as a wedding keepsake with the name of the bride and groom on the label.

Commercial honey in the u.s. tends to play to the association of honey with bears. The now familiar squeezable plastic bear-shaped honey bottle was first invented in 1957, when the founders of Dutch Gold Honey, Ralph and Luella Gamber, came up with the idea. It quickly caught on, and many consumers find it more convenient and less sticky to use than the more traditional honey jar.

The traditional European beehive has influenced popular culture in the United States. The image is an icon of the state of Utah and appears on its flag, even though the state has few bees and produces very little honey. The beehive symbolizes the industry and cooperative nature of the early Mormon pioneers and was chosen by them specifically for those meanings. The beehives' association with productivity is also

Architecture imitates nature: beehive houses in Harran, Turkey.

Architecture patterned on a honeycomb: the Abu Dhabi airport.

alluded to in a saying credited to Abraham Lincoln: 'If you want to gather honey, don't kick over the beehive.'

Not as long lasting, but equally significant during its day, the beehive hairstyle of the 1960s represented the height of attractiveness for many women. Characterized by long hair piled high on top of the head, the fashion required the hair to be carefully teased and formed into elaborate designs, the opposite of the other image of that decade – of free and easy, nature-loving, flower-child youth.

Honey has influenced expressive forms around the world. As its central role in foodways has been usurped by sugar, though, the richness of its symbolism seems also to have declined. Honey has thus moved from a sacred substance to one associated with the pleasantries, but not necessities, of life. Perhaps as appreciation for its benefits is revived, so will its complexity as a symbol and metaphor.

7
The Future of Honey

Honey seems to be coming full circle in its popularity. Although sugar displaced it in the cuisines of modern cultures in the last three to four centuries, it never completely lost its associations with health, medicine, religion and ritual practices that were so prevalent in numerous ancient and early cultures. As often happens, many of those associations survived as folk practices that are now being validated by science. Meanwhile, individuals and groups throughout the world kept up traditions of beekeeping and harvesting honey from the wild, and various social and cultural movements, particularly indebted to the awareness of the interconnected nature of changes to the natural environment, the production of foodstuffs and support for locally sourced work, are supporting a renewed interest in honey.

Concerns about the industrial food system and food safety, philosophical challenges to the dominance of Western attitudes towards food (and life in general), political challenges to free-market capitalism, and the turn towards holistic and natural lifestyles, as well as the expansion of global palates to a more adventurous desire for new tastes, are all contributing to a renewed respect for honey, encouraging people to consume more of it. The shrinking of the world through new media, technologies and increased mobility also means that the wide range of the many honeys' varied flavours is now known and available. This piques people's curiosity, and feeds into an appreciation – and willingness to pay – for speciality honeys as well as for local honeys produced on a smaller and more personal scale. The renewed interest in honey can even be attributed to a rootlessness that seems pandemic in the modern globalized world and that is perhaps eased by consuming foods with strong ties to specific regions, offering eaters a taste of place (*terroir*) that then gives psychological or spiritual grounding.

Unfortunately, there are now concerns about the safety and quality of commercially distributed honey as well as the future of honeybee colonies, and thus of honey production. Disease, pests, mites, loss of habitat, pesticides (particularly neonicotinoids), monocrop agriculture, climate change and the influx of other varieties of bees are threatening colonies in the u.s. and internationally. In 2006–7, American beekeepers reported losses of 30 to 90 per cent of their hives. There were sudden unexplained losses of the worker bees in

The future of honey is tied to local production and consumption.

Honey is increasingly associated with environmentally conscious food production.

spite of relatively healthy amounts of honey and pollen in the hives. This was named Colony Collapse Disorder (CCD) and remains a problem for many beekeepers, not only in the United States but in Europe, too. Scientists have discovered that some garden plants are being grown with neonicotinoids impregnated into the plant's tissue.[1] The insecticides cause neurological impairment in the bees. The bees leave the hives and then cannot find their way back. The common practice of transporting hives from place to place to pollinate particular crops further threatens bee populations by spreading diseases and by facilitating ways for mites to attack the bees. Also, in some locations around the world, traditional methods of obtaining honey from the wild have destroyed nesting sites and colonies.

One response to these concerns has been to create hardier breeds of bee. An example is the Buckfast bee, named after Buckfast Abbey in Devon, where in the early twentieth century one of the monks, Brother Adam, developed a bee that could withstand the parasitic mites that were decimating bee colonies in the British Isles. Starting with English bees and queens imported from Italy, he worked for over seventy years, adding various strains from around the world, to create the Buckfast bee. While Brother Adam's work involved mixing different bees to create new strains, debates abound over the wisdom of using what are considered more intrusive techniques in developing genetically modified bees in order to fight the effects of the pesticides and herbicides prevalent in industrialized agriculture.[2] An example of such experimentation gone wrong is the 'killer bees' of Brazil that are feared to threaten native species as well as the honeybees if they move north, which they might do as temperatures shift due to climate change.

Globalization and neoliberal trade policies have also affected the quality and safety – and taste – of all of our food, including honey. Within the industrial food system, honey has simply become another commodity, to be valued according to the potential profits it can turn.[3] Small producers lose out to larger corporations that can simultaneously sell for cheaper prices and control production and distribution. The quality of the resulting honey tends to be diluted, with consumers opting for lower prices and quantities. The product becomes standardized and homogenized, and the nuances of flavours representing specific places and plant sources are lost. Deception around a product being sold as honey also occurs, since honey itself tends to be more expensive than other sugary substances. In 2013 there were instances of a corn syrup product being sold as honey by Chinese

Honey dripping off a spoon, showing its viscosity.

companies. Such man-made honey is actually not new. In the fifth century BCE the Greek historian Herodotus reported that King Xerxes' army found honey being made of wheat and tamarish, and in Libya the nomadic Gyzantes people made their own honey substitute.[4] Such substitutes can pass for honey among people who have never tasted the real thing or who purchase food only according to price.

Furthermore, within a large, industrial food system, it is easy for people to lose sight of consumer safety or the welfare of the people who work within the industry. Some Chinese honey was found in 2002 to contain an antibiotic, chloramphenicol, which can cause a lethal type of anaemia. Similarly, farmers are pressured into using pesticides and herbicides that can have harmful effects on bees – and the residue can be transferred into the honey, contaminating it.

In response to such concerns, organizations have been established to ensure the quality and sustainability of honey: for example, the American Honey Producers Association, the

Australian Honey Bee Industry Council, the Unique Manuka Factor Honey Association in New Zealand and numerous others around the world. While not focusing on honey, the agricultural industry, as a whole, sees the well-being of bees as crucial since they are used to pollinate major crops, a focus that lends itself to the production of quality honey. Similarly, the issues impacting bees are seen as critical by a number of environmental and governmental groups, including the Natural Resources Defense Council, the European Union (which, in 2013, banned three pesticides known to harm bees), the Environmental Justice Foundation, the Pesticide Action Network Europe, and the u.s.-based Friends of the Earth. The renewed interest in honey – not only as food, but as medicine and cosmetics – can help support these other roles of bees as pollinators.

Does honey have a future? Judging from the wealth of cookbooks now being published, the popularity of beekeeping as a hobby and cottage industry, and the growing awareness of the importance and appreciation of natural foods – and of bees – honey seems to be well positioned for a revival of its earlier significance. Or, as some might say, it looks like honey has a sweet future ahead.

Recipes

Honey can be eaten straight from the beehive or bee's nest without any processing, and many aficionados consider that the best way to fully appreciate its flavour and texture as well as its nutritional benefits. Most of us do not have the opportunity to eat such raw and unfiltered honey, but we do frequently consume honey in an uncooked state – as syrup, sweetener or topping – by itself or mixed with other ingredients. Recipes for using honey, then, can be as simple as the instruction to 'add honey to taste' to more elaborate ones in which honey is used in place of other sugars. In some instances, other flavourings and ingredients are added to the honey itself.

As honey has been so widely used throughout the ages and across the globe, recipes tend to cross between languages, and across religious and cultural boundaries, displaying similarities as well as preserving unique, local heritages. Some recipes have been transformed over time to use sugar instead of honey, but now, thanks to a modern renaissance of interest in natural foods, attention has turned back to honey. To further complicate things, some honey dishes have ritual uses in cultures and older eras, while also being consumed as everyday foods.

Honey beverages have gone through similar transformations, and many have lengthy lineages, especially since honey can be both stirred into other drinks or turned into a drink on its own. Honey, when mixed with water, naturally ferments and can turn into an alcoholic beverage with little to no intervention from human hands – all it needs is water, air and time. To speed up the process and to better control the results, however, honey is usually fermented with a grain or other substances.

Substituting Honey for Sugar in Recipes

For further information, the u.s.-based National Honey Board offers tips for cooking with honey along with recipes on their website (www.honey.com). Honey is sweeter than cane or beet sugar, so not as much is needed to obtain the same amount of sweetness as those foodstuffs. Usually, 260 g (¾ cup) of honey can be substituted for 200 g (1 cup) of sugar.

Honey has very low moisture content (averaging 17.2 per cent) and pulls moisture from the atmosphere, helping to keep baked goods moister than those made with sugar. It also can act as a preservative. Since honey adds moisture, the amount of liquid is usually reduced, sometimes by as much as 120 ml (4 fl. oz) for each 350 g (1 cup) of honey used.

Honey burns more easily than sugar, so baking temperature should be lower – an estimated 15°C (25°F) decrease is usually suggested. Also, if used for basting, water should be added to the pan so that the honey does not burn.

Historical Recipes

Egyptian Honey Cakes

Honey was used as a sweetener and a binder for cakes and breads throughout the ancient world. Flour was made from whatever grains were available, and seeds were frequently added. A drawing on an Egyptian tomb from 1450 BC shows two men frying honey cakes made of date flour. Here is an updated recipe.

3 eggs
220 g (⅔ cup) honey
75 g (½ cup) spelt flour
½ teaspoon vanilla extract or orange (or lemon) zest (optional)

Preheat the oven to 170°C (325°F) and grease a cake pan. Beat the eggs using an electric mixer until a good amount of air bubbles are incorporated. Slowly pour in the honey, and the mixture will begin to thicken. Sift the flour and then gently fold it into the mixture to avoid disrupting the air bubbles. Pour into the prepared cake pan and bake in the preheated oven. Check after 45 minutes. Be careful not to open the door too many times or the cake may fall. The finished cake will be dark brown as a result of the honey. Cooking should be complete at approximately 55 minutes (this can be tested by inserting a toothpick – if it comes out clean, the cake is finished). Cool for ten minutes, remove from pan and drizzle with honey immediately prior to serving. Best served warm.

Greek and Roman Cheesecakes

In the fifth century BC, the Greek playwright Euripides mentioned in his *Cretan Women* 'Cheese-cakes steeped most thoroughly / in the rich honey of the golden bee.' Centuries later Roman cheese-cakes were called *placentae*, and were described by Athenaeus in AD 200 as 'streams of the tawny bee, mixed with the clotted river of bleating she-goats placed upon the flat receptacle of the virgin daughter of Zeus'. The following is a recipe for Roman cheesecake.

140 g (1 cup) plain (all-purpose) flour
325 g (1½ cups) ricotta cheese
1 egg, beaten
1 teaspoon vanilla extract (optional)
4–8 bay leaves
170 g (½ cup) clear honey

Sift the flour into a large bowl. In a separate bowl, beat the cheese until it is soft and creamy. Stir the cheese and egg into the flour, as well as the vanilla extract, if desired. Form a soft dough by kneading on a floured surface and divide into four sections. Mould each section into a bun and place the buns on a greased baking tray with one to two bay leaves under each. Heat the oven to 220°C (425°F). Cover the cakes with a shallow clay pot, a metal bowl or a casserole dish (the Romans used a 'brick', or a domed earthenware cover called a *testo*). Bake for 35–40 minutes, or until golden brown. Heat the honey in a small pan and pour it into the casserole dish that was used as a covering (or a new casserole dish). Place the warm cakes in it so that they absorb the honey. Allow to stand for thirty minutes before serving, flipping the cakes occasionally.

Serves 4

Pasteli (Greek Sesame Seed 'Candy')

Sesame-seed candies like *pasteli* are made today throughout East Asia and the Middle East. Some modern recipes mix brown sugar dissolved in boiling water with the honey. Korean versions use both black and the more common brown sesame seeds.

170g (½ cup) orange blossom honey
225 g (½ lb) sesame seeds
orange water (can be purchased at a speciality food shops,
or plain water may be substituted)

Put the honey in a heavy saucepan and cook over medium heat for fifteen minutes. Stir in the sesame seeds. Continue cooking, stirring constantly, for five minutes. Pour a little orange water on a tray or marble board. Tilt it several times so that the whole tray is moistened. Pour on the honey mixture and spread it to a thickness of 1.25 cm (0.5 in.). Let it cool at room temperature. Cut it into 2.5-cm (1-in.) squares. Turn the pieces with a spatula and let them dry on a rack for two to three hours. Store between layers of greaseproof (waxed) paper in an airtight container.

Makes approx. 36 pieces

Peas à la Vitellius (Peas in an Egg Sauce)

Honey-sweetened sauces were common accompaniments for vegetables, meat and fish for the ancient Romans. The emperor Vitellius reigned for only eight months in the year AD 69, but one of his cooks was the renowned gourmand Apicius. A collection of Roman recipes compiled in the fourth and fifth centuries is credited to him and includes this recipe. Considered the first cookbook, *Apicius* gives a variety of honey sauces that are used for any number of dishes – fish, boiled ostrich, roasted crane, wild boar, cucumbers and many more.

120 ml (4 fl. oz) water

300 g (2 cups) fresh or frozen peas

2 yolks of hard-boiled eggs

½ teaspoon ground black pepper

½ teaspoon ground ginger

¼ teaspoon salt

2 tablespoons honey

1 teaspoon wine vinegar

1 tablespoon oil

Bring the water to a boil. Add the peas and reduce the heat. Simmer, covered, until tender, about fifteen minutes. (If you are using frozen peas, follow the directions on the packet.) If the water boils away during cooking, add more. Drain the cooked peas, cover to keep warm and put aside. While the peas are cooking, mash the egg yolks with the black pepper, ginger and salt. Add the honey, wine vinegar and oil. Beat until smooth. Put the mixture in a small saucepan and bring to a boil. Remove from heat, toss with the peas and serve.

Serves 4

Roman Boiled Eggs with Pine Nut Sauce

60 g (½ cup) soaked pine nuts
pinch of pepper
pinch of lovage (or celery leaf)
1 teaspoon honey
3 tablespoon vinegar
garum fish sauce*
4 medium-boiled eggs

Soak the pine nuts three to four hours beforehand in the vinegar. Mix all the ingredients apart from the eggs thoroughly in a blender. Present this sauce in a sauce boat so that each person can serve himself or herself, pouring the sauce over the sliced eggs.

To make the garum, follow this modern recipe. Cook 1 litre (1 quart) of grape juice, reducing it to one-tenth its original volume. Dilute two tablespoons of anchovy paste in the concentrated juice and mix in a pinch of oregano.

Roman-style Candied Dates

Dates soaked in honey are found throughout the Middle East and the Mediterranean, both historically and in the present. A variation on this recipe is *Dulcia domestica* (Homemade Dessert) in which stoned fresh or dried dates are stuffed with coarsely ground pine nuts, salted, then stewed in honey (or honey-sweetened red wine). They are ready when the outer skins of the dates start to come off.

20 dates
20 whole almonds
black pepper
salt
170 g (½ cups) honey

Remove the stones from the dates. Sprinkle the almonds with freshly ground black pepper and stuff one into each date. Spread a thin layer of salt on a tray. Roll the dates one at a time in the salt. Put them in a heavy saucepan. Pour the honey over the dates and bring to a boil. Reduce the heat and simmer for three minutes. Spoon the warm dates and sauce into individual serving dishes.

Serves 4

Patina de Piris (Pears)

1 kg (2¼ lb) pears, peeled and cored
6 eggs, separated into whites and yolks
ground pepper to taste
½ teaspoon ground cumin
4 tablespoons honey
100 ml (3½ fl. oz) *passum* (a very sweet Roman wine sauce that can be made by boiling down wine or grape juice)
¼ teaspoon salt
olive oil

Preheat oven to 175°C (335°F). Cook the pears until soft, then mash and mix with lightly beaten egg yolks and the pepper, cumin, honey, *passum*, salt and oil. Beat the egg whites until they come to soft peaks, then fold into the pear mixture, put in a casserole and cook for approximately thirty minutes in the oven. Serve with a little pepper sprinkled on the top.

Serves 8–10

Sarda Ita Fit (Cooked Tuna, adapted from *Apicius*)

500 g (1 lb 2 oz) tuna fillet
½ teaspoon ground pepper
½ teaspoon thyme
½ teaspoon oregano
½ teaspoon rue
150 g (1 cup) chopped dates
1 tablespoon honey
50 ml (2 fl. oz) white wine

2 tablespoons wine vinegar
2–3 tablespoons green olive oil
4 hard-boiled eggs, quartered, for the garnish.

Sauté the tuna until the flesh begins to flake and it is cooked all the way through, then mash it together with the other ingredients. Garnish with the egg quarters and serve.

Serves 4

Indian Honey and Sesame Fritters

Honey plays a special role in Indian culture. According to legends, the Buddha ate honey balls after he obtained enlightenment. At another time, a monkey brought him honeycomb while he was in the forest meditating to bring peace to quarrelling factions of his followers. These fritters could also be baked into ball shapes.

2 teaspoons honey, extra honey for drizzling
150 g (1 cup) plain (all-purpose) flour
240 ml (8 fl. oz) water
oil (for frying)
1 teaspoon baked sesame seeds

Mix the honey and the flour in a bowl and add enough water to create a thick batter consistency. Heat the oil in a frying pan and drop in some batter. Flip over, frying both sides to a golden colour. Place golden fritters onto a platter lined with an absorbent paper, such as a paper towel. Continue frying the remaining batter the same way, until all the batter is used. When all batter is used, drizzle with extra honey and top with sesame seeds. Serve immediately.

Serves 2

Gulab Jamun

70 g (½ cup) dry milk powder
40 g (⅓ cup) plain (all-purpose) flour
½ teaspoon baking power
two pinches of ground cardamom
2 tablespoon ghee (clarified butter), melted
160 ml (⅔ cup) warm milk
340 g (1 cup) honey
1 teaspoon rosewater (optional)
approximately 240 ml (1 cup) water
oil for frying

Mix milk powder, flour, baking powder and one pinch of cardamom together in a large bowl. Mix in melted butter and then add milk, combine until well blended. Let rest for twenty minutes, covered. In the meantime, combine honey, water, rose water and a pinch of cardamom in a skillet. Allow to simmer until honey and water are blended; then remove from heat and set aside. In another skillet, add oil until it is halfway full. Heat this skillet over medium heat for approximately five minutes. Knead the dough and form it into approximately twenty balls. Lower the temperature under the skillet and drop the balls in, frying in two separate batches. After about five minutes, the colour will not have changed significantly, but the balls should rise to the top of the oil and enlarge to twice their original size. Once the balls are floating, increase the temperature to a medium setting and turn the balls until they are golden brown in colour. Once golden, remove from oil and place on an absorbent sheet, allowing to cool slightly. Once all balls are fried, add them into the syrup skillet and simmer for five minutes over medium heat. Squeeze the balls like a sponge, causing them to absorb the syrup. Serve warm or chilled.

Frumenty

Porridges, made of any grain available, were a basic everyday food throughout Europe and the Middle East, particularly among peasants. They could be 'fancied up' for special occasions, as in this recipe. Honey was frequently drizzled onto porridge and bread, as it still is today. Flatbreads cooked on griddles (pancakes) were common in the Middle Ages and easier than baking. Honey might be mixed with cinnamon for a topping.

360 ml (¾ cup) milk
½ teaspoon almond extract
2 tablespoon honey
150 g (1 cup) cracked wheat
1 egg yolk
ground saffron (optional)

Mix the milk, almond extract and honey in a heavy saucepan. Bring to a boil. Add the cracked wheat and reduce the heat to low. Cover and cook, stirring occasionally until the liquid is absorbed, about fifteen minutes. Remove from the heat. Stir in the egg yolk. Add a pinch of saffron and mix well. Serve hot or cold.
Serves 4

Spice Cakes and Gingerbread

Used with permission from www.theoldfoodie.com, an excellent website for historical sources of recipes. From Thomas Austin, *Two Fifteenth-century Cookery-books* (London, 1888). Harleian MS. 279 & Harl, MS. 4016, with extracts from Ashmole MS. 1429, Laud MS. 553, & Douce MS 55)

Early spice cakes (otherwise known as gingerbread) were very different from modern-day spice cakes. They were usually hard and made of dough that had sat for several months so that the honey in it would ferment. They were frequently shaped by hand or in moulds, and were decorated with dough. They appeared in several varieties throughout Europe – the French *pain d'épice*,

German *Lebkuchen*, Belgian *couques de Dinant* and Dutch *taai-taai*. There were also honey biscuits called Nurembergers, named after the German city that was an ancient centre for the spice trade. Interestingly, many original recipes used leftover breadcrumbs, as in the following fifteenth-century recipe for 'Gyngerbrede'.

> Take a quart of honey and sethe it and skime it clene; take Safroun, pouder Pepir and throw theron; take gratyd Brede and make it so chargeant that it wol be y-lechyd; then take pouder canelle and straw ther-on y-now; then make it square, lyke as thou wolt leche yt; take when tho lechyst hyt, an caste Box leves a-bowyn, y-stykyd ther-on, on clowys. An if thou wold have it Red, colour it with Saunderys y-now.

'Gingerbrede'

Another recipe adapted from original medieval recipes:

340 g (1 cup) honey
1 teaspoon ground ginger
1/8 teaspoon ground cloves
1/8 teaspoon ground cinnamon
¼ teaspoon white pepper and pinch saffron (optional)
170 g (1½ cup) dry breadcrumbs
1 tablespoon anise (fennel) seeds

Warm the honey on a very low heat. Add all the spices except the anise seeds and stir to blend. Add the breadcrumbs and mix thoroughly. Cover and cook over a medium heat until thick (about fifteen minutes). Place the dough on a flat service and either press into a square or rectangle about 2 cm (0.75 in.) thick or mould into small shapes. Sprinkle the anise seeds on top, pressing gently into the dough with the side of a knife. Allow to cool, thinly slice if desired, then cover. (It may need to be refrigerated.) Serve at room temperature.

Douce Ame (Capon in Milk and Honey)

As in ancient Rome, honey frequently sweetened sauces for meat for Europeans in the Middle Ages. It helped preserve the meat and also gave it a prized golden colour.

1 capon (3.5 kg (7–8 lb)) or 2 chickens (1.5 kg (3–4 lb each), cut into pieces
140 g (1 cup) flour
½ teaspoon salt
½ teaspoon black pepper
110 g (¼ cup) oil
720 g (3 cups) milk
170 g (½ cup) honey
3 tablespoons chopped parsley
½ teaspoon ground sage
1 teaspoon ground savory
1 teaspoon ground saffron (optional)
100 g (⅔ cup) chopped walnuts

Put the capon or chicken pieces in a strong bag with flour, salt and pepper. Shake until well coated. Heat the oil in a large frying pan. Add and brown the chicken pieces on both sides. Mix the milk, honey, parsley, sage, savory and saffron. Pour over the browned chicken or capon pieces in the frying pan. Cover, reduce heat and simmer for one to one and a half hours over a very low heat. Remove the frying pan from the heat and transfer the chicken (or capon) and sauce to a serving platter. Sprinkle the walnuts over the chicken.
Serves 6–8

Cameline Sauce

This sauce from fourteenth-century England and France was used on meat and fish. It differs from the capon recipe above in that the honey is boiled with other ingredients, including breadcrumbs, before it is poured over meat or fish.

⅛ teaspoon crushed red pepper
720 ml (3 cups or 1¼ pints) beef stock or broth
3 tablespoons honey
1 tablespoon wine vinegar
2 cinnamon sticks
½ teaspoon whole cloves
½ teaspoon ground ginger
½ teaspoon whole black peppercorns
½ teaspoon ground mace
75 g (1½ cups) fresh wholewheat bread, crumbled
salt
ground cinnamon

Put the crushed red pepper, beef stock, honey, wine vinegar, cinnamon sticks, whole cloves, ginger, black pepper and mace in a heavy saucepan. Bring to a boil. Reduce the heat and simmer, covered for fifteen minutes. Add the crumbled bread and cook over a low heat, stirring occasionally, for thirty more minutes. Pour the sauce through a strainer, carefully pressing out all the liquid. Discard the bread. Add salt to taste. Pour into a gravy boat, sprinkle lightly with ground cinnamon and serve with the roasted meat.

Beef and Potato *Tzimmes*
National Honey Board, www.honey.com, used with permission.
Adapted measurements.

2 tablespoons vegetable oil, divided
0.9 kg (2 lbs) stewing beef, cut in 2.5–4 cm (1–1½ in.) chunks
300 g (2 cups) chopped onion
300 g (2 cups) sliced carrots, 2.5 cm (1 in.) thick
2 teaspoons garlic salt
300 g (2 cups) cubed potato, 2.5 cm (1-in.) thick
300 g (2 cups) cubed sweet potato, 2.5 cm (1-in.) thick
110 g (⅓ cup) honey
½ teaspoon ground cinnamon

⅛ teaspoon ground pepper
120 g (¾ cup) dried apricots
120 g (¾ cup) pitted prunes
2 tablespoons flour, optional
2 tablespoons chopped parsley

Heat 1 tablespoon of oil in a heavy 5-litre (4-quart) pot over medium heat. Add the beef and brown on all sides. Remove the beef from the pan, add the remaining oil, if necessary, and sauté the onion until tender. Return the beef to the pan; add the carrots, salt and about 960 ml (4 cups) water to cover ingredients. Bring to a boil, reduce heat, cover and simmer for one hour. Add the potatoes, sweet potatoes, honey, cinnamon and pepper; stir and return to a boil. Reduce the heat and simmer, partially covered, for thirty minutes or until potatoes are barely cooked. Add the dried fruit and simmer, uncovered, for thirty minutes or until beef is tender. The liquid should be slightly thickened. If necessary, dissolve the flour in 3 tablespoons of water and stir into the stew; return to a simmer, stirring frequently. Sprinkle with the parsley before serving.

Serves 4

Modern Recipes

As in ancient and medieval times, honey continues to be used in cakes and breads, particularly in Eastern European cultures and for special occasions. Russian and Ukrainian honey cakes often include walnuts and apples, and are made for the three harvest festivals in August, known as the three saviours: 14 August celebrates the first day for harvesting honey; 19 August is for apples and other fruits; and 29 August is for nuts. Many of these cakes are layered with a dairy-based filling. Jewish culinary traditions are similar and feature honey as an ingredient and as a symbol of the sweetness of life.

Lekekh

From the Jewish American cook and food scholar Eve Jochnowitz, who claims that buckwheat honey gives this traditional Jewish honey cake its distinctive flavour. See www.inmolaraan.blogspot.com, used with permission.

Sift dry ingredients together:
900 g (6 cups) plain (all-purpose) flour (you may use part or all wholewheat pastry flour)
1 scant tablespoon ginger
1 tablespoon cinnamon
3/8 teaspoon ground cloves (3 cloves)
several scrapings of nutmeg
400 g (2 cups) sugar
2 tablespoons baking powder
1 teaspoon baking soda
75 g (½ cup) cocoa

Blend together in processor or blender:
2 oranges (remove seeds and cores, use peel and pulp)
50 g (¼ cup) ginger preserves
340 g (1 scant lb or about 1 ½ cups) buckwheat honey
325 g (1 ½ cups) oil
2 teaspoons vanilla
2 tablespoons slivovitz
8 eggs (added at last minute)

Stir together:
25 g (1 oz) dark (semisweet) chocolate, chopped
50 g (2 oz) unsweetened chocolate, chopped
2 tablespoons instant coffee
120 ml (½ cup) boiling water

Stir the chocolate and coffee into the orange mix, then mix into the dry ingredients. Fold in three grated apples (large, Macintosh-type). Bake in three or four cake tins, walnuts on top, at 230°C

(450°F) for five minutes, then 200°C (400°F) for five minutes, then 180°C (350°F) for twenty minutes. Test for doneness. Makes three large cakes, three dozen cupcakes or four medium-sized cakes. This cake benefits from resting, unrefrigerated, for one day, especially if you use wholewheat flour. It will keep for more than two weeks without refrigeration.

Honey Vanilla Kernik
Eve Jochnowitz offers this almost raw, vegan 'cheesecake' for the 'joyous festival of *peysekh*'.

150 g (1 cup) raw cashews
75 g (½ cup) hemp seeds
85–170 g (¼–½ cup) bamboo honey or other flavourful honey, to taste
2 tablespoons coconut oil
¼ teaspoon salt (2 fat pinches)
2 tablespoons agar-agar (kanten)
seeds from one vanilla bean
1 (15-cm (6-in.)) pastry crust

Soak the cashews and hemp seeds overnight. Drain them and add 360 ml (13 fl. oz) fresh water, the honey, oil and salt, and blend at high speed for several minutes. Heat the blended nut mixture with the agar until the agar dissolves and pour into a 15-cm (6-in.) springform pan with or without a prepared crust. You could also pour the mixture into individual cups or bowls and leave to set.

Baklava
Used with permission from Sue Manos's family recipe.

Baklava is found throughout Turkey and the Middle East, as well as in some Eastern European cultures, where it tends to be more of a cake and made with wheat flour.

For the baklava:
900 g (2 lb or 9½ cups) ground walnuts
200 g (1 cup) sugar
1½ tablespoon cinnamon
340 g (¾ lb or 3 sticks) butter, melted
¼ teaspoon ground cloves
3–8 drops orange extract
900 g (2 lb) filo (phyllo) dough, thawed but kept in refrigerator
until ready to use (do not microwave to thaw)

For the syrup:
400 g (2 cups) sugar
450 ml (2 cups) water
680 g (2 cups) honey
2 cinnamon sticks
juice of one orange or lemon
grated peel of the orange or lemon

Mix the ground nuts with sugar and spices. Grease a 33 × 23 cm
(9 × 13 in.) tin. Layer ten sheets of filo into the tin, spreading
butter generously between every two layers. Put on half of the
nut mixture. Layer a few more sheets of filo/butter and then add
the rest of the nut mixture. Layer eight to ten more sheets of filo,
with butter on the very top layer. Before baking, cut into the size
squares you want, cutting those squares in half to form triangles.
You only have to cut though the top few layers. (This is because
you will not be able to cut through the cooked, crispy top layers
after it is baked without the filo crumbling.) Bake at 175°C (350°F)
for 45 minutes or until golden brown. While the baklava is baking, cook the syrup by boiling all the ingredients for ten minutes.
Transfer to a cool pan, remove cinnamon sticks and cool well.
Many people strain out the grated orange or lemon peel, but this
is optional. When the baklava is done, pour cold syrup onto the
hot baklava. Let sit until the syrup has soaked in and the baklava
has cooled down.

Southern Rice Pudding with Honey

This is an approximation of the recipe I grew up with in the American South (North Carolina) and is adapted from memories of my grandmother and mother, both of whom were wonderful cooks, who frequently cooked without the benefit of written recipes. The dish was a childhood favourite and continues to be a comfort food. It is an excellent way to use leftover rice and can be used for other grains as well as noodles.

Either use 320 g (1½ cups) of cooked rice or cook 200 g (1 cup) of white or brown rice in 450 ml (2 cups) of water. Preheat oven to 170°C (325°F). Beat three eggs and combine with 450 ml (2 cups) of milk, 170 g (½ cup) of honey, one teaspoon vanilla and half a teaspoon of salt. Mix well, then stir in the rice and 50 g (⅓ cup) of raisins. Pour into a glass baking dish or individual serving-size glass cups and bake for thirty minutes. Stir and grate a little nutmeg or sprinkle cinnamon on top. Bake for another thirty minutes. The pudding is ready when a knife inserted into the middle comes out clean. Refrigerate. (Tip from my mother: hide individual servings in back of refrigerator, so that they are not all eaten immediately!)

Granola

Iconic of the 1960s back-to-the-land social movement and often associated today with 'hippy' lifestyles and environmentalists, granola was invented for medical purposes in 1863 in Dansville, New York, at Jackson Sanitarium by Dr Connor Lacey. Dr John Harvey Kellogg also developed a similar cereal, called 'granula'. The recipe below is versatile and can be adapted with whatever substitutions are desired.

270 g (2½ cups) rolled oats
3 tablespoons brown sugar
½ teaspoon cinnamon
¼ teaspoon salt

110 g (⅓ cup) honey
60 ml (¼ cup) vegetable oil
1 teaspoon vanilla extract
100 g (½ cup) dried fruit, diced
75 g (½ cup) nuts or seeds, toasted and chopped

Stir together the oats, sugar, cinnamon and salt. Combine the honey, oil and vanilla and pour over the oats. Mix all together and thinly spread on a baking sheet. Bake for twenty minutes at 150°C (300°F). Stir occasionally. Add fruit and nuts and stir. Pour onto a flat, oiled surface to cool. Break into small pieces and store in an airtight container.

Honey-glazed Ham

A popular meal for Easter dinners in the United States.

1 2.5 kg (5-lb) ham (pre-cooked)
25 g (¼ cup) whole cloves
160 g (¼ cup) dark corn syrup
680 g (2 cups) honey
150 g (⅔ cup) butter

Heat the oven to 170°C (325°F). Make the glaze from the honey, butter and syrup in a double boiler. Score the ham and put the cloves in. Place the ham in the oven and baste with the glaze every ten to fifteen minutes until the ham is heated through the centre, about 50 minutes. Turn on the grill (broiler) for the last five minutes to caramelize the glaze.
Serves 15

Other glaze recipes for meats, poultry, fish, vegetables and even fruit include the following.

300 g (1½ cups) light brown sugar
170 g (½ cup) clover honey

or

320 ml (1 cup) orange juice
125 g (½ cup) mustard (preferably whole grain)
85 g (¼ cup) honey

or

60 g ml (¼ cup) cider vinegar
170 g (½ cup) honey
1 teaspoon Worcestershire sauce
3 tablespoons unsalted butter
3 tablespoons chopped thyme

Cook the glaze ingredients in a saucepan over medium heat until smooth. Pour over dishes while cooking.

Honey-crusted Salmon or Chicken

4 salmon fillets or chicken breasts
salt and ground pepper
4 tablespoons plain (all-purpose) flour
170 g (½ cup) honey
2 tablespoons olive oil

Season the fillets/breasts. Use one tablespoon of flour and one tablespoon of honey for each fillet/breast. Dredge in flour, then drizzle with honey. Sear in olive oil on both sides over medium heat for two minutes each. Then, either cover the pan, lower the heat and allow to cook for six to eight minutes or bake at 200°C (400°F) uncovered until done, eight to ten minutes.
Serves 4

Teriyaki Honey Chicken

National Honey Board, www.honey.com, used with permission

170 g (½ cup) honey
140 g (½ cup) soy sauce
60 g (¼ cup) sherry wine
1 teaspoon grated fresh ginger
2 cloves garlic, crushed
1 1.5 kg (3 lb) broiler-fryer chicken, cut up

Place chicken in a plastic food storage bag or large glass baking dish. Combine the remaining ingredients in a small bowl and pour over the chicken, turning to coat. Close the bag or cover the dish with plastic wrap. Marinate in refrigerator for at least six hours, turning two or three times.

Remove the chicken from the marinade; reserve the marinade. Arrange the chicken on a rack over a foil-lined pan. Cover the chicken with foil. Bake at 175°C (350°F) for thirty minutes. Uncover and brush with marinade. Bake, uncovered, for 30–45 minutes or until done, brushing occasionally with marinade. You may substitute 2 teaspoons ground ginger for the fresh ginger.
Serves 4–6

Lamb and Dried Fig Tagine

National Honey Board, www.honey.com, used with permission

3 tablespoons olive oil
150 g (1 cup) onion, chopped
1 teaspoon Moroccan spice blend (*ras el hanout*)
½ teaspoon ground turmeric
½ teaspoon ground cinnamon
¾–1 kg (½ to 2 lb) lamb sirloin, trimmed and cubed
(2.5 cm/1 in.)
½ teaspoon salt
freshly ground black pepper
1 425 g (15 oz) can diced tomatoes with juice

½ cup unsalted chicken stock
12 dried mission figs, prunes or apricots
150 g (1 cup) carrot, cut into 1 cm (0.5 in.) pieces
2 tablespoons honey
1 tablespoon diced preserved lemon, or 1 teaspoon finely chopped lemon zest
2 tablespoons coriander (cilantro), finely chopped

Heat the olive oil in a large Dutch oven or a braising pan. When it is hot enough to sizzle an onion, add the onion, Moroccan spice blend, turmeric and cinnamon. Cook, stirring, for about five minutes, or until the onions are translucent. Add the lamb and sprinkle with the salt and a generous grinding of pepper. Cook the meat, turning, for about five minutes, or until lightly browned. Add the tomatoes and chicken stock and bring to the boil. Reduce the heat to low, cover and cook for thirty minutes. Add the figs and carrot. Cover and cook for about thirty minutes longer, or until the meat is tender. Stir in the honey and lemon. If there is too much liquid, turn the heat to high and boil for about five minutes, or until the liquid is reduced. Taste the sauce and add more salt and pepper if needed. Sprinkle with coriander and serve.
Serves 4

Honey-glazed Carrots

This is a favourite recipe from the author's family in the southern United States. It was usually made at holidays, particularly Thanksgiving.

500 g (1 lb) carrots, sliced lengthwise or baby ones, cooked
1 tablespoon butter
2 tablespoons honey
1 tablespoon lemon juice
salt
ground black pepper
¼ cup parsley, chopped, for garnish

Cook the carrots, butter, honey and lemon juice in a covered saucepan over medium heat until a glaze forms. Season with salt and pepper and garnish with the parsley.
Serves 4

Mexican Honey-glazed Winter Squash

I once had honey-glazed squash for dessert at a restaurant in Pueblo, Mexico, where it was garnished with edible roasted crickets. The squash was flavoured with cinnamon, but many modern recipes call for the addition of chilli peppers to give it the spiciness associated with Mexican cuisine. This recipe probably has ancient origins.

1 1-kg (2-lb) winter squash (1 large or 2 small banana, Hubbard, butternut or acorn)
60 g (¼ cup or ½ stick) butter
¼ tablespoon honey
1 tablespoon orange rind
salt to taste
¼ teaspoon cinnamon
¼ teaspoon ground chilli pepper (optional)

Wash and cut the pieces of squash into serving size, removing all seeds and unwanted members. Place on a baking tray, rind side down. Bake at 190°C (375°F) until tender, about 25 minutes. Melt the butter in a saucepan over low heat. Add the honey, salt and grated orange rind. Pour onto the squash pieces, sprinkle on cinnamon and pepper, and bake for ten minutes, or more to glaze.
Serves 8

Honey-braised Red Cabbage

The sweet and sour flavour of this cabbage is typical of Pennsylvania Dutch, Amish and German American foodways. Other vegetables can be prepared this way as well. Green beans, pearl onions and carrots are favourites.

1 tablespoon butter
1 tablespoon olive oil
1 red onion, sliced thin
1 green apple, sliced thin
1 head red cabbage, core removed and sliced thin
60 ml (¼ cup) cider vinegar
1 teaspoon sea (kosher) salt
1 teaspoon cracked black pepper
2 tablespoons honey

In a large saucepan heat the butter and olive oil over medium heat. Add the onion and cook for three minutes. Add the apple and cabbage, and cook for five minutes. Stir in the vinegar, salt, pepper and honey. Cover and cook for twenty minutes, stirring occasionally, until the cabbage is soft.

Honey Coleslaw

1.4 kg (18 cups) cabbage, finely chopped (about 1 head)
30 g (¼ cup) carrot, shredded (1 medium carrot)
2 tablespoons minced sweet onions
120 g (½ cup) mayonnaise
110 g (⅓ cup) honey
2 tablespoons milk
2 tablespoons buttermilk
1½ tablespoons white vinegar
2½ tablespoons lemon juice
½ teaspoon sea (kosher) salt
⅛ teaspoon fresh ground pepper

Chop the cabbage, carrot and onion into very small pieces and set aside. In a large bowl, combine the remaining ingredients and beat until smooth. Add the vegetables and mix well. Cover and refrigerate for at least two hours before serving (do not skip this step, as the flavour needs time to 'set' into the slaw).

Honey Mustard Dipping Sauce

190 g (¾ cup) Dijon mustard
120 g (½ cup) mayonnaise
90 g (¼ cup) honey
¼ teaspoon ground red pepper
1/8 teaspoon garlic salt

Simply stir together the ingredients and serve with hot or cold meats and vegetables (raw or cooked).

Honey BBQ Sauce

60 g (¼ cup or ½ stick) butter or margarine
1 medium onion, diced, about 150 g (1 cup)
340 g (1 cup) ketchup
80 ml (⅓ cup) water
90 g (¼ cup) honey
2 tablespoons lemon juice
1 tablespoon Worcestershire sauce
¼ teaspoon ground black pepper

Melt the butter in pan, add the onion and sauté until tender. Add the rest of the ingredients and bring to a boil. Reduce the heat and simmer for five minutes, stirring often.

Mead

The most basic and traditional mead recipe is simply honey and water left in the open air to ferment. The process can take a long time, however, and is not guaranteed to turn into a palatable drink, so yeast is usually added by modern mead makers to accelerate the fermentation. Most recipes call for a yeast developed especially for mead, but other substances can be substituted, including champagne yeast, freeze-dried wine, yeast nutrient and more. Beer-brewing equipment can be used, or the tools improvised. The flavour of the mead depends on the flavour of the honey used, so choose accordingly. Also, the more honey used, the higher the alcohol content will be, and that content is generally higher than beer.

5.5–8 kg (12–18 lb) honey
8–9 l (4–4½ gallons) water (tap, bottled or spring water is recommended)
¼ oz. yeast (or 5 teaspoons yeast nutrient, 5 teaspoons yeast energizer and 2 packets yeast)

Boil the water. Remove from heat and add the honey, stirring until honey is dissolved. Let cool for about half an hour (until cool to touch). Meanwhile, dissolve the yeast in a covered cup of lukewarm water. Pour the cooled honey water into the container being used for fermentation, then stir in yeast. Cover and let ferment for two weeks to one month, when carbon-dioxide bubbles occur once a minute. Siphon the mead to the second fermentation container and let it age for at least one month. Once it is clear, it is ready to siphon into bottles to age further.

Variations can be added during the primary or secondary fermentation. Examples include:

Add 4 pears, 4 cinnamon sticks and 230 g (½ lb) raw ginger root

Use 8 l (2 gallons) apple juice (cider) in place of water
Add 450 g (16 oz) frozen strawberries or 340 g (12 oz)

frozen blueberries, and 450 g (16 oz) peach purée to a mead made with orange blossom honey. (Fruit meads are frequently called 'melomels'.)

A handful of hops can be added to the boiled water to counter the sweetness of the honey.

References

1 Honey's Sweet History

1 The first date is suggested by 'Study Finds Honey Bees Originated from Asia not Africa', www.entomologytoday. org, 25 August 2014, while the latter comes from Mark L. Winston, *Bee Time: Lessons From the Hive* (Cambridge, MA, 2014), p. 5.

2 Tammy Horn, 'Honey Bees: A History', www.newyorktimes.com, 11 April 2008.

3 Jaime Henderson, 'How Bees Came Buzzing to Los Angeles', www.kcit.org, 3 March 2014.

4 Peggy Trowbridge Filippone, 'Honey History', www.about.com, accessed 17 March 2015.

5 Stephen L. Buchmann and Banning Repplier, *Letters from the Hive: An Intimate History of Bees, Honey, and Humankind* (New York, 2005), p. 121.

6 Ibid., p. 124.

7 Vedic hymn quoted ibid, p. 123.

8 More can be read and viewed about honey rituals on numerous Internet websites, for example, www.thaibuddhist. com.

9 Holley Bishop, *Robbing the Bees: A Biography of Honey, the Sweet Liquid Gold that Seduced the World* (New York, 2005), p. 45.

10 Aristotle quoted ibid., p. 45.

11 Quoted ibid., p. 49.

12 Quoted Buchmann with Repplier, *Letters from the Hive*, p. 213.
13 'Medieval Beekeeping', www.medievalists.net, 21 June 2015.
14 Kim Flottum, *The Backyard Beekeeper's Honey Handbook: A Guide to Creating, Harvesting, and Cooking with Natural Honeys* (Beverly, MA, 2009), p. 8.
15 Bee Wilson, *The Hive: The Story of the Honeybee and Us* (New York, 2006), p. 161.
16 Sydney Mintz, *Sweetness and Power: The Place of Sugar in Modern History* (New York, 1985).
17 Food and Agricultural Organization of the United Nations, 'Value-added Products from Beekeeping', www.fao.org, Section 2.5.1, accessed 17 March 2015.
18 Winston, *Bee Time*, p. 22.

2 Busy as a Bee:
Honey Production and Harvesting

1 Keith S. Delaplane, *First Lessons in Beekeeping* (Hamilton, IL, 2007), p. 6.
2 Ibid., p. 12.
3 Sue Hubbell, *A Book of Bees: And How to Keep Them* (New York, 1988), p. 78.
4 Stephen Buchmann with Banning Repplier, *Letters from the Hive: An Intimate History of Bees, Honey, and Humankind* (New York, 2005).
5 Karen Hursh Gruber, 'Honey: A Sweet Maya Legacy', www.mexconnect.com, 2 April 2009.
6 Eva Crane, *The World History of Beekeeping and Honey Hunting* (New York, 1999).
7 Hilda M. Ransome, *The Sacred Bee in Ancient Times and Folklore* (New York, 2004), p. 27.
8 Buchmann with Repplier, *Letters from the Hive*, p. 47.
9 Ransome, *The Sacred Bee*.
10 Dylan M. Imre, Lisa Young and Joyce Marcus, 'Ancient Maya Beekeeping (ca. 1000–1520 CE)', *University of Michigan*

Undergraduate Research Journal, VII (2010), http://deepblue.lib.
umich.edu, accessed 10 December 2015.

11 St Bernard, *Honey and Salt: Selected Spiritual Writings of Bernard
of Clairvaux* (Visalia, CA, 2007).

12 See www.honey.com for more information on the National
Honey Board. Also see 'Status Report on the Health of the
U.S. Honey Bee Industry', www.usda.gov, 14 August 2013.

13 'Honey' (ISSN 1949-1492), National Agricultural Statistics
Service (NASS) Agricultural Statistics Board, U.S. Department
of Agriculture, www.usda.gov, 20 March 2015.

14 The U.S. Department of Agriculture and the U.S.
Environmental Protection Agency, '2013 Report on
the Stakeholder Conference on Honey Bee Health',
www.extension.org, 3 May 2013.

3 Main Course and Dessert: Honey as Food

1 Stephen Buchmann with Banning Repplier, *Letters from the
Hive: An Intimate History of Bees, Honey, and Humankind*
(New York, 2005), p. 170.

2 Lucille Recht Penner, *The Honey Book* (New York, 1980),
p. 97.

3 Holley Bishop, *Robbing the Bees: A Biography of Honey, the
Sweet Liquid Gold that Seduced the World* (New York, 2005),
p. 185.

4 Elizabeth Birchall, *In Praise of Bees: A Cabinet of Curiosities*
(Shrewsbury, 2014).

5 Martin Grassberger et al., eds, *Biotherapy: History, Principles,
and Practice* (New York, 2013).

6 Bee Wilson, *The Hive: The Story of the Honeybee and Us*
(New York, 2006), p. 152.

7 Ibid., p. 175.

8 Grace Pundyk, *The Honey Trail: In Pursuit of Liquid Gold and
Vanishing Bees* (New York, 2010).

9 Colin Turnbull, *The Forest People* (New York, 1961).

10 The term 'vegan' was coined by Donald Watson, 1944; quoted in 'Why Honey is Not Vegan', www.vegetus.org/honey/honey, accessed 17 March 2015.

11 Hattie Ellis, *Honey: A Complete Guide to Honey's Flavours and Culinary Uses with over 80 Recipes* (New York, 2014), pp. 174–86.

12 Quoted in Birchall, *In Praise of Bees*, p. 154.

13 From Emily Dickinson, *Collected Poems* (Boston, MA, 1924), Book III, XII.

14 For details on the grading of honey, see 'USDA Honey Grading', www.honeytraveler.com, accessed 17 March 2015.

4 The Nectar of the Gods: Honey as Drink

1 Holley Bishop, *Robbing the Bees: A Biography of Honey, the Sweet Liquid Gold that Seduced the World* (New York, 2005), p. 181.

2 Stephen Buchmann with Banning Repplier, *Letters from the Hive: An Intimate History of Bees, Honey, and Humankind* (New York, 2005), p. 143.

3 See www.barnonedrinks.com, accessed 2 April 2015.

4 Bee Wilson, *The Hive: The Story of the Honeybee and Us* (New York, 2006), p. 156.

5 P. E. McGovern et al., 'Fermented Beverages of Pre- and Proto-historic China', *Proceedings of the National Academy of Sciences of the United States of America*, CI/51 (6 December 2004), pp. 17593–8.

6 Bishop, *Robbing the Bees*, p. 179.

7 William Pokhlebkin, *A History of Vodka* (New York, 1992), p. 12.

8 Ibid.

9 Claire Preston, *Bee* (London, 2006).

10 Bishop, *Robbing the Bees*, p. 178.

11 'Not Just for Renaissance Fairs: Mead Producers Triple in 10 Years', www.huffingtonpost.com; see 'Mead: Fastest

Growing Segment in U.S. Alcohol Industry',
www.meadist.com.

12 Bee Wilson, for example, describes her distaste for it, in
The Hive, p. 159.

13 Joyce Miller, 'The Bee's Lees: A Collection of Mead
Recipes' (1994), www.brewery.org/brewery/library/
beeslees, accessed 2 April 2015.

5 Honey for Health and Healing

1 See 'Medicinal Uses of Honey', www.webmd.com, accessed
17 March 2015.

2 Bee Wilson, *The Hive: The Story of the Honeybee and Us*
(New York, 2006), p. 203.

3 Stephen Buchmann with Banning Repplier, *Letters from the
Hive: An Intimate History of Bees, Honey, and Humankind*
(New York, 2005), p. 123.

4 Wilson, *The Hive*, p. 198.

5 Summarized and quoted from Buchmann with Repplier,
Letters from the Hive, p. 213.

6 Joseph Patrick Byrne, *Daily Life During the Black Death*
(Westport, CT, 2006), p. 58.

7 Apiservices – Beekeeping Virtual gallery, 'Dark Honey
has More Illness-fighting Agents than Light Honey',
www.beekeeping.com, accessed 10 February 2016.

8 See 'Medicinal Uses of Honey', www.webmd.com, accessed
17 March 2015.

9 P. H. Kwakman et al., 'How Honey Kills Bacteria',
www.ncbi.nim.nih.gov, accessed 17 March 2015.

10 Manisha Deb Mandal and Shyamapada Mandal, 'Honey:
Its Medicinal Property and Antibacterial Activity', *Asian
Pacific Journal of Tropical Biomedicine*, 1/2 (April 2011),
pp. 154–60, www.ncbi.nlm.nih.gov, accessed 20 March 2015.

11 M. I. Khalil et al., 'Antioxidant Properties of Honey and
its Role in Preventing Health Disorder', *Open Neutraceuticals
Journal*, III (2010), pp. 6–16.

12 Mandal and Mandal, 'Honey'.

13 Farshad Hasanzadeh Kiabi et al., 'Can Honey be Used as an Adjunct in Treatment of Post Tonsillectomy Pain?', *Anesthesiology and Pain Medicine*, IV/5 (December 2014), www.ncbi.nlm.nih.gov, accessed 17 March 2015.

14 Michael Murray, Joseph Pizzorno with Lara Pizzorno, *The Encyclopedia of Healing Foods* (New York, 2005), p. 649.

15 See www.beesource.com, accessed 17 March 2015.

16 See www.foodsafety.gov, accessed 17 March 2015.

17 Wilson, *The Hive*, pp. 195–200.

18 Murray, Pizzorno with Pizzorno, *The Encyclopedia of Healing Foods*.

19 Buchmann with Repplier, *Letters from the Hive*, p. 137.

20 James A. Kelhoffer, *The Diet of John the Baptist: Locusts and Wild Honey in Synoptic and Patristic Interpretation* (Mohr Siebeck, 2005), p. 90.

21 Ibid., p. 87.

22 Wilson, *The Hive*, p. 210.

23 Joe Traynor, *Honey: The Gourmet Medicine* (Bakersfield, CA, 2002), p. 35.

6 Honey as Art and Symbol in Folk and Popular Culture

1 For example, see www.honey-health.com.

2 Tova Forti, 'Bee's Honey: From Realia to Metaphor in Biblical Wisdom Literature', *Vetus testamentum*, LVI/3 (July 2006), pp. 327–41.

3 Stephen Buchmann with Banning Repplier, *Letters from the Hive: An Intimate History of Bees, Honey, and Humankind* (New York, 2005), p. 167.

4 Elizabeth Birchall, *In Praise of Bees: A Cabinet of Curiosities* (Shrewsbury, 2014), p. 163.

5 Ibid., p. 164.

6 Buchmann with Repplier, *Letters from the Hive*, p. 133.

7 See 'Honey', at www.etymonline.com.

8 For a translation from the Russian, see www.russian-crafts.com.
9 More information can be found on the group's website: www.sweethoneyintherock.org.
10 To view the pot, see the antique dealer Peter Szuhay, www.peterszuhay.com.

7 The Future of Honey

1 For reports about some of the latest information on bees, see D. van Engelsdorp et al., 'Colony Collapse Disorder: A Descriptive Study', *PLoS One*, IV/8 (2010): e6481; Marge Dwyer, 'Study Strengthens Link Between Neonicotinoids and Collapse of Honey Bee Colonies', 9 May 2014, Harvard School for Public Health, www.hsph.harvard.edu.
2 Current issues and solutions are explored by Charles C. Mann, photos by Anand Varma, 'Quest for a Superbee', *National Geographic* (May 2015), pp. 84–101.
3 Stephen Buchmann with Banning Repplier, *Letters from the Hive: An Intimate History of Bees, Honey, and Humankind* (New York, 2005), p. 147.
4 Elizabeth Birchall, *In Praise of Bees: A Cabinet of Curiosities* (Shrewsbury, 2014), p. 152.

Select Bibliography

Atkins, Edward Laurence, and Roy A. Grout, *The Hive and the Honey Bee: A New Book on Beekeeping Which Continues the Tradition of 'Langstroth on the Hive and the Honeybee'* (Hamilton, IL, 1975)

Birchall, Elizabeth, *In Praise of Bees: A Cabinet of Curiosities* (Shrewsbury, 2014)

Bishop, Holley, *Robbing the Bees: A Biography of Honey, the Sweet Liquid Gold that Seduced the World* (New York, 2005)

Buchmann, Stephen, with Banning Repplier, *Letters from the Hive: An Intimate History of Bees, Honey, and Humankind* (New York, 2005)

Columella, *De re rustica* (Bologna, 1504)

Crane, Eva, ed., *Honey, A Comprehensive Survey* (New York, 1975)

——, *The World History of Beekeeping and Honey Hunting* (New York, 1999)

Delaplane, Keith S., *First Lessons in Beekeeping* (Hamilton, IL, 2007)

Ellis, Hattie, *Honey: A Complete Guide to Honey's Flavors and Culinary Uses with over 80 Recipes* (New York, 2014)

Flottum, Kim, *The Backyard Beekeeper's Honey Handbook: A Guide to Creating, Harvesting, and Cooking with Natural Honeys* (Beverly, MA, 2009)

Frisch, Karl Von, *The Dancing Bees: An Account of the Life and Senses of the Honey Bee* (New York, 1955)

Horn, Tammy, *Bees in America: How the Honey Bee Shaped a Nation* (Lexington, KY, 2005)

Hubbell, Sue, *A Book of Bees: And How to Keep Them* (New York, 1988)

Jones, Richard, and Sharon Sweeney-Lynch, *The Beekeeper's Bible: Bees, Honey, Recipes & Other Home Uses* (New York, 2011)

Masterton, Laurey, *The Fresh Honey Cookbook / 84 Recipes from a Beekeeper's Kitchen* (New York, 2013)

Nasi, Andrea, Ilaria Rattazzi, and Franz Rivetti, *The Honey Handbook: An Introduction to New and Exciting Uses for Nature's Most Perfect Food* (New York, 1978)

Nordhaus, Hannah, *The Beekeeper's Lament: How One Man and Half a Billion Honey Bees Help Feed America* (New York, 2011)

Penner, Lucille Recht, *The Honey Book* (New York, 1980)

Pinto, Maria Lo, *The Honey Cookbook: Recipes for Healthy Living* (New York, 1993)

Pundyk, Grace, *The Honey Trail: In Pursuit of Liquid Gold and Vanishing Bees* (New York, 2010)

Radošević, Petar, 'Honey in Roman Culture', *Bee World*, LXXX-VI/3 (2010), p. 58.

Ransome, Hilda M., *The Sacred Bee in Ancient Times and Folklore* (New York, 2004)

Readicker-Henderson, E., and Ilona, *A Short History of the Honey Bee: Humans, Flowers, and Bees in the Eternal Chase for Honey* (Portland, OR, 2009)

Root, A. I., *The ABC and XYZ of Bee Culture: A Cyclopedia of Everything Pertaining to the Care of the Honey-bee; Bees, Hives, Honey, Implements, Honeyplants, Etc.* (Medina, OH, 1917)

Rusden, Moses, *A Further Discovery of Bees: Treating of the Nature, Government, Generation & Preservation of the Bee: With the Experiments and Improvements Arising from the Keeping them in Transparent Boxes, Instead of Straw-hives: Also Proper Directions (to All Such as Keep Bees) as Well to Prevent their Robbing in Straw-hives, as their Killing in the Colonies* (London, 1679)

Sammataro, Diana, and Alphonse Avitabile, *The Beekeeper's Handbook* (Ithaca, NY, 1998)

Schacker, Michael (foreword by Bill McKibben), *A Spring without Bees: How Colony Collapse Disorder has Endangered our Food Supply* (Guildford, CT, 2008)

Traynor, Joe, *Honey: The Gourmet Medicine* (Bakersfield, CA, 2002)

Wilson, Bee, *The Hive: The Story of the Honeybee and Us*
    (New York, 2006)

Wilson-Rich, Noah, Kelly Allin, Norman Carreck and Andrea
    Quigley, *The Bee: A Natural History* (Princeton, NJ, 2014)

Winston, Mark L., *Beetime: Lessons From the Hive*
    (Cambridge, 2014)

Journals and Periodicals

American Bee Journal

Bee Culture

Bee World

Gleanings in Bee Culture

Modern Beekeeping

Websites and Associations

A Brief History of Honey
www.honeyassociation.com

American Beekeeping Association
www.abfet.org

American Honey Producers Association
www.ahpanet.com

American Mead Makers Association
http://mead-makers.org

Apiservices, Virtual Beekeeping Gallery
www.beekeeping.com

Bee News: Kingston Beekeeper's Magazine
www.kingstonbeekeepers.org.uk

Dadant & Sons
www.dadant.com

Peggy Trowbridge Filippone, 'Honey History'
www.about.com.homecooking

Food and Agricultural Organization of the United Nations (FAO)
www.fao.org

Value-added Products From Beekeeping
www.fao.org/docrep/w0076e/w0076e04.htm
.

Hive and Honey Apiary
www.hiveandhoneyapiary.com

Honey Association (UK)
www.honeyassociation.com

Honey Traveler: Everything in the world about honey
www.honeytraveler.com

National Honey Board
www.honey.com

Acknowledgements

I owe a huge debt for this book to Susan Eleuterio, folklorist, community activist and expert beekeeper. Sue wrote much of Chapter Two on honey production and contributed her knowledge of honey and her keen editorial eye to the rest of the manuscript as well. Her enthusiasm encouraged me in my research and writing, and her friendship continues to be invaluable.

Andrew Smith, the Edible series editor, encouraged me not only to write this book but to pursue food as a scholarly subject before it was trendy to do so. In the mid-1990s there were only a handful of us studying food. We listened to each other's tales of discovery and woe, and provided affirmation in believing that our work was important. Andy was always an enthusiastic supporter, and I appreciate his encouragement.

Family also played a part in writing this book. Many memories of times with my father revolved around food, particularly in the southern Appalachians – where he was from and where I loved going back to visit with him. We would traipse through the woods and fields of those mountains, usually ending somewhere with a meal that frequently involved local honey. My children have also each contributed in their own way. Hannah liked exploring and would gamely tag along on outings and field trips. She also sacrificed her time by trying out various cosmetics and skin care products made with honey. Will applied his honey-tongued wit to paintings of bees and other fancies, brought a sweet and sunny disposition to life in general, and Ian lent me his expertise in biology, botany and nutrition by looking over portions of this book. He was also my excuse for purchasing speciality buckwheat honeys known for their medicinal properties. With all of them, memories of their childhoods are as sweet as honey for me.

Photo Acknowledgements

The author and publishers wish to express their thanks to the below sources of illustrative material and/or permission to reproduce it. Some locations of artworks are also given below, in the interests of brevity.

Achillea (reproduced under the terms of a GNU General Public License – full licensing terms can be found at https://www.gnu.org/licenses/gpl.html): p. 18; photos by or courtesy of the author: pp. 8, 19, 62, 66, 68, 73, 98, 101, 133; photo Biswarup Ganguly (licensed under the Creative Commons Attribution 3.0 Unported license): p. 20; British Museum, London: p. 23; photo Lance Cheung/ U.S. Department of Agriculture (licensed under the Creative Commons Attribution 2.0 Generic license): pp. 48–9; photo CBW/ Alamy Stock Photo: p. 122; photo DucDigital (licensed under the Creative Commons Attribution-NoDerivs 2.0 Generic license): p. 70; photo R. B. Fleming: p. 23; FreeImages.com/AYakuban: p. 27; FreeImages.com/Corey Mathews: p. 54; FreeImages.com/ huhu: p. 14; FreeImages.com/MadMaven/T. S. Heisele: p. 36; FreeImages.com/Mamat Bilang: p. 135; FreeImages.com/Philip Niewold: p. 130; photo Carol M. Highsmith (Carol M. Highsmith Archive, Library of Congress, Washington, DC, Prints and Photographs Division): p. 128; photo Shannon Holman (reproduced under the terms of a Creative Commons Attribution 2.0 Generic licence): p. 58; photo Charles Hose/Wellcome Library, London (reproduced under the terms of a Creative Commons Attribution

Index

italic numbers refer to illustrations; **bold** to recipes